AFF

De aedibus international

Die Inspirationen und die architektonische Kultur einzelner Architekten in Europa zu dokumentieren und zusammenzuführen, das ist das Ziel der Reihe *De aedibus international*. So können wir seit 2009 architektonische Brennpunkte der jüngeren europäischen Architekturgeschichte wie etwa London, die Beneluxstaaten, Deutschland, Österreich und Südtirol mit einzelnen Bänden erreichen. Die Reihe wird in ihrer Kontinuität gleichsam zu einem Gedächtnis der Architektur, das die Werke dem Vergessen entzieht. Von allen der mit hohem Qualitätsanspruch ausgewählten Architekturschaffenden werden die wichtigsten Bauten festgehalten, ausführlich dargestellt und dokumentiert. Jeder Band dient auch der Reflexion über den architektonischen Willen, der hinter den Projekten steht. So sind in dieser Reihe bereits etliche namhafte Kritikerinnen und Kritiker aus verschiedenen Ländern zu Wort gekommen.

Der Hauptteil in jedem Band widmet sich dagegen der Welt der Anschauung. So sind jeweils anhand von Bildern und Plänen einige bemerkenswerte Bauten dargestellt, die nicht einer routinierten «Produktion» entsprungen sind. Vielmehr steht hinter jedem Entwurf eine leidenschaftliche Auseinandersetzung mit der Aufgabe und deren Prämissen.

Heinz Wirz
Verleger

De aedibus international

The *De aedibus international* series aims to document and compile the inspirations and architectural culture of individual architects in Europe. Since 2009, we have published individual volumes on hotspots of European architectural history such as London, the Benelux countries, Germany, Austria and South Tyrol. Such continuity allows the series to become a form of architectural memory, ensuring that the architecture is not forgotten. The most important buildings by each of the selected high-quality architects are presented, described in detail and documented. Each volume also serves to reflect upon the architectural motivation behind the projects. Thus the series includes numerous articles by renowned critics from various countries.

However, the core of each book is dedicated to the world of observation. Images and plans present a number of remarkable buildings that are not the result of routine "production". Instead, each design stems from a passionate engagement with the task and its premises.

Heinz Wirz
Publisher

21 De aedibus international

AFF – Berlin/Lausanne

QUART

Hartmut Frank
FIRMITAS – AUF DER SUCHE NACH EINER
WIEDERGEWINNUNG VON DAUERHAFTIGKEIT IM BAUEN   6

SCHUTZHÜTTE, TELLERHÄUSER   14

HAUS LINDETAL, MECKLENBURG-VORPOMMERN   20

WOHNBLOCK ELF FREUNDE, BERLIN   26

TAUFZENTRUM KIRCHE ST. PETRI-PAULI, LUTHERSTADT EISLEBEN   32

UMNUTZUNG HAUPTGÜTERBAHNHOF, HANNOVER   38

STADTWERKSTATT, BERLIN   44

SÄCHSISCHE LANDESAUSSTELLUNG, ZWICKAU   50

SPORE INITATIVE, BERLIN   56

WERKVERZEICHNIS   62

BIOGRAFIEN   64

BIBLIOGRAFIE   66

AUSSTELLUNGEN, PREISE, BIOGRAFIE AUTOR   68

Hartmut Frank
FIRMITAS – IN SEARCH OF REGAINING DURABILITY IN ARCHITECTURE   7

MOUNTAIN HUT, TELLERHÄUSER   14

LINDETAL HOUSE, MECKLENBURG-WEST POMERANIA   20

"ELF FREUNDE" HOUSING BLOCK, BERLIN   26

CHRISTENING CENTRE, ST. PETRI-PAULI CHURCH, EISLEBEN   32

CONVERSION OF THE MAIN FREIGHT RAILWAY STATION, HANOVER   38

URBAN WORKSHOP, BERLIN   44

SAXON STATE EXHIBITION, ZWICKAU   50

SPORE INITIATIVE, BERLIN   56

LIST OF WORKS   63

BIOGRAPHIES   65

BIBLIOGRAPHY   67

EXHIBITIONS, AWARDS, AUTHOR'S BIOGRAPHY   69

FIRMITAS – AUF DER SUCHE NACH EINER WIEDERGEWINNUNG VON DAUERHAFTIGKEIT IM BAUEN

Hartmut Frank

Nicht die fotogene Sprengung der sozialen Wohnungsbauten von Pruitt Igoe von 1972, die Charles Jencks kurz darauf zum Symbol einer von ihm und anderen gerade ausgerufenen Postmoderne verklärt hat, möchte ich meiner kurzen Vorbemerkung zu diesem Band einer Auswahl von Arbeiten des Berliner Büros AFF voranstellen, sondern die undatierte Aufnahme eines frühen Autofriedhofs in den Vereinigten Staaten mit übereinander getürmten Ford-T-Automobilen, sowie die Zeichnung zu einem Transportband in den Schlachthöfen von Chicago, die Sigfried Giedion 1948 in seinem Buch *Mechanization Takes Command* der Fliessbandfertigung des Ford T gegenübergestellt hat.

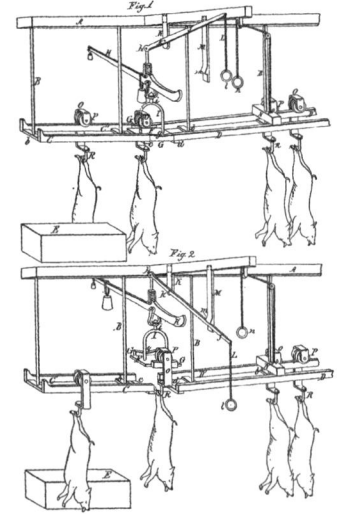

Einer der folgenreichen Träume der Moderne war die Fliessbandproduktion von Wohnhäusern als zwar kurzlebiges, aber für alle erschwingliches Konsumprodukt. Überlegungen dieser Art bedeuteten das Ende jedweder Architektur für eine kunstsinnige Elite. An ihre Stelle sollte das rationellste Bauen für alle treten, Massenproduktion statt individueller Kunst. Der Siegeszug von Frederick Taylors wissenschaftlich geplanten und kontrollierten Produktionsprozessen und Fords Massenproduktion radikal vereinfachter Automobile wiesen den Weg in eine bessere Zukunft. Le Corbusier riet 1923 in seiner Kampfschrift *Vers une architecture* gleich in mehreren Kapiteln mit der Überschrift «Des yeux, qui ne vois pas» den «Herren Architekten», doch bitte einmal hinzuschauen und die Tendenzen der Zeit endlich zur Kenntnis zu nehmen und in ihr Entwurfsrepertoire zu integrieren. Während Walter Gropius und Ernst May gern selbst zu «Wohnfords» geworden wären, war Sigfried Giedion bescheiden genug, lediglich die minimierten Reihenhäusern J.J.P. Ouds in Rotterdam als «Wohnfords» zu bezeichnen. 1948 lieferte er in seinem Buch *Mechanization takes Command* die faszinierende Geschichte des technischen Fortschritts nach, mit der er seine Erwartungen an die serielle Grossproduktion von Bauwerken historisch verankern wollte.

Fliessbandproduktion (aus: Giedion: *Mechanization Takes Command*. 1948)
Mass production line (from: Giedion, *Mechanization Takes Command*, 1948)

Das Neue Bauen des 20. Jahrhunderts sollte sich von den Zwängen der Vitruv'schen Forderung von *utilitas*, *venustas* und *firmitas* freimachen und sich die Verheissungen einer Wegwerfproduktion mit ihrer geplanten Obsoleszenz zu eigen machen. Aus Vitruvs Trias fand nur noch die *utilitas* die volle Gnade dieser Bauprophesten. Die *venustas*, die Schönheit, degenerierte zu einem quasi automatischen Nebenprodukt der Nützlichkeit gemäss Sullivans Diktum *form follows function* und die *firmitas* wurde mehr als Standfestigkeit im statischen Sinne, denn als Dauerhaftigkeit interpretiert.

Die Dogmen des Neuen Bauens waren zwar zu keinem Zeitpunkt kritiklos hingenommen worden, aber sobald sie in der zweiten Hälfte des 20. Jahrhunderts in Ost und West unübersehbar das Baugeschehen dominierten, stiessen sie auf zunehmend stärkeren Widerspruch. Diese Kritik war uneinheitlich, heterogen und pauschal, weshalb sich die Versuche, die durch sie beförderten baulichen Gegenmodelle als Postmoderne unter einem gemeinsamen Label abzulegen, als voreilig und kontraproduktiv erwiesen. Die Kritik betraf städtebauliche Qualitäten, Fragen der Ästhetik, formale Einfallslosigkeit und die Kurzlebigkeit der verwendeten Materialien. Sie entzündete sich meist an der monotonen Einfachheit und Schmucklosigkeit der Bauten und reichte bis zur Klage über das völlige Verstummen der Architektur als künstlerischer Ausdrucksform der Gegenwartskultur. Gegenüber architektonischen Qualitäten, die fraglos auch das Neue Bauen hervorgebracht hatte, blieb sie blind und überliess diese widerspruchslos der Abrissbirne. Die durch den Paradigmenwechsel bewirkten Neuerungsansätze

FIRMITAS –
IN SEARCH OF REGAINING DURABILITY IN ARCHITECTURE

Hartmut Frank

Ford-T-Schrottplatz
Ford Model T junkyard

Instead of the photogenic demolition of the Pruitt Igoe social housing estate in St. Louis, Missouri in 1972, which Charles Jencks proceeded to turn into a symbol of the postmodernism that he and others had just proclaimed, I wish to precede my brief introductory text for this volume of selected works by the Berlin architectural office AFF with an undated photograph of an early "graveyard for automobiles" in the United States, depicting piles of Model T Fords, as well as the sketch of a conveyor belt in the slaughterhouses of Chicago, with which Sigfried Giedion compared the Model T production line in his 1948 book *Mechanization Takes Command*.

One of the momentous dreams of Modernity was the automated production of housing as a short-lived, but affordable consumer product. Such considerations implied the end of all architecture for an artistically minded elite. It was to be replaced by the most rational building: mass production instead of individual art. The triumphant advances made by Frederick Taylor's scientifically planned and controlled production processes, combined with Ford's mass production of radically simplified automobiles, paved the way for a better future. In 1923, Le Corbusier wrote his combative book "*Vers une architecture*", heading several chapters with the words "*Des yeux, qui ne vois pas*", asking "MM. Les architectes" to take a closer look and finally acknowledge the trends of the times, integrating them into their design repertoire. While Walter Gropius and Ernst May themselves aspired to become "the Fords of housing", Sigfried Giedion was modest enough to simply name the minimal terraced houses by J.J.P. Ouds in Rotterdam "*Wohnfords*" ("*housing Fords*"). In 1948, he followed it up with his book entitled *Mechanization Takes Command*, an account of the history of technical progress, with which he aimed to historically anchor his expectations in the large-scale serial production of buildings.

The Neues Bauen movement in the 20th Century was aimed at liberating architects from the constraints of the Vitruvian laws of *utilitas*, *venustas* and *firmitas*, instead exploiting the promise of disposable production with its planned obsolescence. Of the Vitruvian triad, only *utilitas* enjoyed the full support of these building prophets. *Venustas*, beauty, was degenerated into a quasi-automated by-product of usefulness in accordance with Sullivan's maxim of "form follows function", while *firmitas* was interpreted more as stability in the sense of statics, rather than durability.

The dogmas of Neues Bauen had never been accepted without criticism, but they encountered stronger opposition as soon as they became obviously dominant both in the East and West in the second half of the 20th century. The criticism was inconsistent, heterogeneous and generalised, which is why attempts to throw all the critics' proposed counter-models into one basket and label them "postmodern" proved to be premature and counterproductive. The criticism also addressed urban-planning qualities, questions of aesthetics, a lack of formal imagination and the short-lived nature of the materials used. They were mainly incensed by the monotonous simplicity and indecorous nature of the buildings, even going as far as complaining about the complete silencing of architecture as a form of artistic expression in contemporary

mussten ebenso heterogen bleiben wie diese Kritiken. Während einige Architektinnen und Architekten versuchten, eine neue Materialökologie oder einen Bezug zu tradierten Typologien und regionalen Formtraditionen zu entwickeln, bemühten sich andere um die Wiedergewinnung von städtebaulichen und landschaftlichen Kontexten oder flüchteten sich in gewagte Konstruktionen beziehungsweise in freie künstlerische Fantasien. Die Projektauswahl des vorliegenden Bandes verweist uns auf den Umgang des Büros AFF mit der Problematik einer als Dauerhaftigkeit verstandenen *firmitas*, auf Fragen der Materialwahl, der Variation von herkömmlichen Typologien und den Umgang mit überkommenen Fragmenten von Formen und Bildern, mit dem langen Leben der Formen. Hier sollen aber nicht die in der Folge vorgestellten Arbeiten vorausgreifend kommentiert werden, sondern zu deren besserem Verständnis anhand einiger Beispiele lediglich Vermutungen zur Genese der spezifischen Entwurfsauffassung angestellt werden, die ihnen zugrunde liegen könnte.

Schon in der unmittelbaren Nachkriegszeit hatten die Fragen um die Wiederverwendung der Schuttmassen der zerbombten Städte als Baumaterial und als Gestaltungselement grosse Bedeutung erhalten. Erinnert sei hier nur an Otto Bartnings Bauprogramm für evangelische Notkirchen in ganz Deutschland, bei dem vorgefertigte Holzbinder mit Mauerwerk aus Trümmerschutt ausgefacht wurden. Und natürlich an Rudolf Schwarz' monumentale Kirche Sankt Anna in Düren, die nach Abbruch der neogotischen Ruine als geschlossener Mauerwerksbau aus dem Schutt errichtet wurde und statt über Fenster durch eine Wandfläche aus Glasbausteinen belichtet wurde. Nur selten wurden die Ruinen als Ausgangspunkt einer Neugestaltung aufgegriffen wie bei der Frankfurter Paulskirche von Schaupp, Blanck, Schwarz und Krahn oder bei der Alten Pinakothek in München von Hans Döllgast, die weder Rekonstruktion noch Neubau waren, sondern die Ruine zum entscheidenden formalen Ausgangspunkt für die neue Nutzung machten. In der Regel ging in diesen Jahren die Auseinandersetzung um originalgetreue Rekonstruktion von Vorgängerbauten wie beim Dresdener Zwinger und beim Frankfurter Goethehaus; oder um den spurenlosen Abriss von durchaus noch reparablen Ruinen wie etwa der Berliner Reichskanzlei und diversen Schlössern in Hannover, Braunschweig oder Berlin – und selbst von Vorzeigeobjekten des Neuen Bauens wie Mendelsohns Columbushaus am Potsdamer Platz in Berlin oder seinem gänzlich unzerstörten Kaufhaus Schocken in Stuttgart.

Die Weiternutzung zerstörter oder aus der Nutzung gefallener Bauten reicht weit in die Geschichte zurück. Sie war angesichts der Kosten von Baumaterial eher die Regel als die Ausnahme. Um einen Totalabbruch zu rechtfertigen, bedurfte es gravierender religiöser, militärischer oder machtpolitischer Gründe, die eher ideologischer als technischer Natur waren. Erinnert sei hier nur an die beeindruckenden Spuren römischer Amphitheater in mehreren Ländern um das Mittelmeer, zum Beispiel in Lucca oder in Arles, an zu Kirchen umgebaute griechische Tempel wie in Siracusa, oder an die sehr frei restaurierten und umgenutzten mittelalterlichen Burgen, die an vielen Orten Europas zu finden sind.

Der Gedanke, Ruinen früherer Epochen zur Lieferung von Baumaterial zu verwenden, ist noch verbreiteter als die Umnutzung. Erst jüngeren Datums ist die Weiterverwendung von Industrieabfällen für den Bau von Strassen und Häusern. So hat die Bewohner zahlloser Slums in der Dritten Welt ihren Erfindungsreichtum bei der Nutzung von Wellblech, Ölfässern und dergleichen bewiesen. Aber erst die Hippies schafften es in den 1960er Jahren, eine ernsthafte Architekturdiskussion über die Weiterverwendung von sonst nutzlosem Müll anzuregen. In den Aussteigerkommunen von Colorado und New Mexiko schweisste Steve Baer mit seinen Genossinnen und

Pfarrkirche Sankt Anna, Düren
1. Vorkriegszeit
2. Zerstörung, 1944
3. Aufbau, Rudolf Schwarz, 1954–1956

St. Anna Church, Düren
1. Pre-war period
2. Destruction, 1944
3. Reconstruction, Rudolf Schwarz, 1954–1956

Das befestigte Amphitheater von Arles, 1686
The fortified amphitheatre of Arles, 1686

culture. They remained blind to architectural qualities that certainly also existed in the architecture of Neues Bauen, and left it to the wrecking ball without protest. The approaches to renewal that developed as a consequence of this paradigm shift were inevitably as heterogeneous as the criticism itself. While some architects attempted to develop a new ecology of the material or establish a relationship to traditional typologies, others tried to regain the context with urban and landscape-planning. Other alternatives escaped into audacious constructions or free artistic fantasies. The selection of projects presented in this volume demonstrates the way the office AFF approaches the problem of *firmitas*, which is grasped as durability, as well as the choice of materials, the variation of standard typologies and the stance towards traditional fragments of forms and images, towards the longevity of forms. However, this introduction does not intend to anticipate comments on the works presented in this book. Instead, to understand the work better, it will outline a few examples to propose assumptions on the genesis of the specific design concept that might underlie it.

Even in the immediate aftermath of World War II, questions concerning the reuse of enormous volumes of rubble in bombed out cities, both as building material and as design elements, were very important. One notable example worth recalling in this context is Otto Bartning's construction programme for 84 emergency churches throughout Germany, in which prefabricated wooden trusses were filled in with war-induced debris. Similarly, Rudolf Schwarz' compact St. Anna church in Düren was completely constructed out of the stones from the demolished Gothic Revival ruin, replacing even the windows with a wall made of glass bricks to provide natural light. It was rare to pick up on thethe ruins as a starting point for redesign, as was the case with Frankfurt's Paulskirche by Schaupp, Blanck, Schwarz and Krahn, or the Alte Pinakothek in Munich by Hans Döllgast, which were neither reconstruction measures nor new buildings. Instead, they made the ruin the decisive formal starting point for the new use. During those years, the prevailing approach was either to produce an identical reconstruction of the previous building, as in the cases of the Zwinger in Dresden and the Goethe House in Frankfurt, or to completely demolish ruins that could have been repaired, as was the fate of the Reich Chancellery in Berlin and various palaces in Hanover, Braunschweig and Berlin, but also of prime examples of Neues Bauen, such as Mendelsohn's Columbushaus on Potsdamer Platz in Berlin or his completely undamaged Schocken department store in Stuttgart.

The practice of continuing to use buildings that are either damaged or obsolete has a long history. In view of building-material costs, it tended to be the rule rather than the exception. To justify a complete demolition, there had to be considerable religious, military or power-political reasons, which were more of an ideological rather than a technical nature. One need only recall the impressive remains of Roman amphitheatres in several Mediterranean countries, such as in Lucca or in Arles, or also Greek temples that have been converted into churches, as in Siracusa, or even the very freely restored and converted medieval castles that can be found in many places throughout Europe.

The idea of using ruins from former ages as providers of building materials is even more widespread than their conversion. The continued use of industrial waste to build roads and houses is relatively new. For instance, the residents

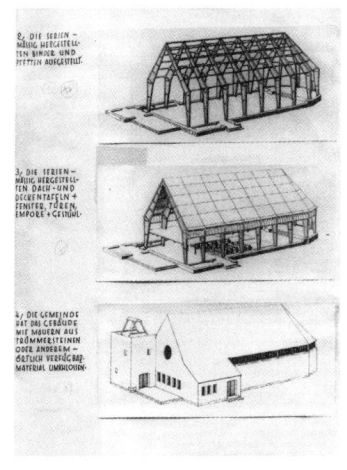

Bauprinzip der Notkirchen, Otto Bartning, 1949
Emergency-church construction principle. Otto Bartning, 1949

Genossen Mitte der 1960er Jahre vor allem aus Automobilschrott die ersten *Mini-Buckies* zusammen, für die er publikumswirksam geodätischen Kuppelkonstruktionen nutzte wie sie Buckminster Fuller zuvor für das US-amerikanische Militär entwickelt hatte. Dank der *Whole-Earth Kataloge* machten diese *Mini-Buckies* schnell weltweit Karriere und inspirierten nicht nur die Londoner Archigram-Gruppe, sondern auch experimentierfreudige Architekten wie Lucien Kroll, der in Belgien aus industriell hergestellten, aber ungenutzt entsorgten Türen, Fenstern und Wandelementen kostengünstig die Universitätsgebäude von Louvain-la-Neuve bei Brüssel, Klosteranlagen und Privathäuser errichtete und damit zu einem der frühen Gurus ökologischen Bauens in Europa wurde.

Titelblatt Steve Bear, 1969
Front page, Steve Bear, 1969

Von diesen Arbeiten war der gedankliche Schritt zu Kunstobjekten wie dem *Plattenpalast* der Berliner Architekten Wiewiorra, Hopp, Schwark nicht weit. Dieser fand allerdings erst 2005 statt, als sie mit einer Projektgruppe der TU Berlin die Montage eines Objektes aus vorgefertigten Platten der Serie WBS 70 eines zurückgebauten Wohnblocks in Berlin-Marzahn erproben konnten. 2009 stellten sie es schliesslich als Veranstaltungsort – ergänzt um Originalfenster des abgebrochenen Palastes der Republik – in einem Berliner Privatgarten als eine Art minimalistisches Konzept-Art-Objekt auf.

Alle bisher zitierten Beispiele qualifizieren sich bezüglich der Dauerhaftigkeit allein durch die Weiternutzung von Ruinen, die Wiederverwendung von Materialien aus Bauschutt und Industriemüll sowie ungenutzten oder überflüssig gewordenen Elementen des aktuellen Baubetriebs. Sie berührten noch nicht die Fragen nach der ästhetischen und der sinngebenden Dimension der Baukunst, die das Neue Bauen wenn nicht komplett negiert, so doch stark in den Hintergrund gedrängt hatte; noch nicht die Fragen der gebauten Umwelt, der Einbindung in städtebaulichen Kontext, typologische Traditionen und in die Landschaft und den jeweiligen Naturraum. Erst die Beschäftigung der Architektenschaft mit der Dauerhaftigkeit und Langlebigkeit von Formen, Bildern und Narrativen kann auch diese Dimension der Nachhaltigkeit erschliessen. Als Versuche und Anregungen in dieser Richtung sollen die folgenden Arbeiten des Büros AFF gesehen und verstanden werden.

Im Gefolge des Rückbaus von industriell vorgefertigten Grosssiedlungen in Schweden, Frankreich und der ehemaligen DDR, wo hierfür extra staatliche Sonderförderprogramme wirksam wurden, entstanden mehrere Projekte, zum Teil in Entwicklungsländern, bei denen demontierte Platten erneut verwendet wurden. Diese erhoben nur selten den Anspruch, einen Beitrag zur Baukultur zu leisten und vermieden auch die ironische Kritik am Traum vom fordistischen Wohnungsbau, der hinter dem *Plattenpalast* noch zu erkennen ist.

AFF hatten bereits vor dem eher als Konzeptkunstwerk, denn als Architektur zu deutenden *Plattenpalast* bei ihren ersten Bauten mit einer Wiederverwendung von Bauelementen aus der Hochzeit der industriellen Vorfertigung einen Ansatz verfolgt, der sich von der wortwörtlich verstandenen Wiederbenutzung von Abbruchmaterial deutlich absetzte und gestalterische Ziele verfolgt, ohne dabei architekturideologisch oder gesellschaftspolitisch werten zu wollen. Kurz nach der Jahrtausendwende liessen sie für ihr Haus Zivcec in der Mustersiedlung Neues Bauen am Horn in Weimar plastische Formsteine – wie sie zu DDR-Zeiten vielfach in Kooperation von in den Bereichen Design, Bildhauerei und Architektur Tätigen entwickelt und bei vielen Bauten verwendet worden waren – neu produzieren und zu einer Formsteinwand montieren, die sie ihrem Einfamilienhaus als sinnstiftendes Element einfügten. Hierdurch erzeugten sie einen weiter gefassten Bezug zur Vorgeschichte dieses Quartiers, als es das naheliegende Anknüpfen an Gestaltungsansätze beim benachbarten Haus am Horn von 1923 und an die Dogmen des Bauhauses hätte leisten können.

of countless slums in Third World countries have demonstrated their ingenuity using corrugated iron, oil barrels and the like. However, the hippies in the 1960s were the first to encourage serious architectural discussion on the reuse of otherwise useless waste. In the mid-60s drop-out communes of Colorado and New Mexico, Steve Baer and his comrades welded junk together, mainly from cars, to produce the first *minibuckies*, creating visually striking geodetic dome constructions, as Buckminster Fuller had previously built for the US military. Thanks to the Whole Earth Catalogues, these *minibuckies* quickly became popular around the world, not only inspiring the London Archigram Group but also architects eager to experiment such as Lucien Kroll in Belgium: he used industrially manufactured, but obsolete wall, door and window elements to develop cheap university buildings for Louvain-la-Neuve near Brussels, as well as monasteries and private homes, thereby becoming an early guru of ecological building in Europe.

It is only a small conceptual step from those works to pieces of art such as the *Plattenpalast* by the Berlin architects Wiewiorra, Hopp and Schwark. But it was only taken in 2005, as they worked together with a project group from the TU Berlin to assemble a structure made of prefabricated WBS-70 panels from a dismantled housing block in Berlin-Marzahn. By 2009 they were finally able to set this up in a private garden in Berlin, supplemented by original windows of the demolished Palast der Republik, as a venue for events, as a kind of minimalist concept art object.

All the examples mentioned above only gain the quality of durability through the continued use of ruins, the reuse of materials from building rubble and industrial waste, or elements that are no longer used or have become superfluous in the current building process. They did not yet address questions of an aesthetic or meaningful dimension of architecture, which Neues Bauen did not completely negate, but had very much forced into the background. Nor did they address aspects of the built environment, integration into the urban-planning context, typological traditions, the landscape and the respective natural environment. It is only possible to tap into that dimension of sustainability when architects also study the durability and longevity of forms, images and narratives. The following selection of works by the office AFF should be regarded as attempts at and inspiration in moving in this direction.

Following the demolition of major prefabricated estates in Sweden, France and the former GDR, where special state support programmes for that purpose became effective, several projects were set up some of them in developing countries, in which dismantled panels were reused. These only rarely claimed to make a contribution to building culture and of course avoided any ironic criticism of the dream of Ford-like housing development as was still apparent in the *Plattenpalast*.

This last example can be regarded more as a work of art than of architecture. But even earlier, AFF referred to building elements from the heyday of industrial prefabrication when working on their first buildings. Yet the approach clearly set itself apart from the literally understood reuse of demolition material and pursued design goals without wanting to evaluate them from an architectural, ideological or socio-political point of view. Shortly after the turn of the millennium, for their *Zivcec House* in the model settlement Neues Bauen am Horn in Weimar, they used sculpturally formed

Wohnhaus Zivcec mit Formsteinwand «Halbschale», Weimar, 2006
Zivcec residential building with "Half shell" shaped-stone wall, Weimar, 2006

Der hier erkennbare Umgang mit Zeit und Form, mit materiellem Relikt und ideellem Konzept ist im Werk von AFF keine einmalige Episode und auch alles andere als zufällig. Er deutet auf ein konstituierendes, wenn nicht *das* zentrale Moment ihres Verständnisses von Nachhaltigkeit und Dauerhaftigkeit des Bauens hin. Es zielt darauf ab, bei der Lösung gestalterischer Fragen ihre Wahrnehmung und Erinnerung mit der Konstruktion und Funktion einer Bauaufgabe konzeptionell und formal in Einklang zu bringen. Das zeigen ihre Arbeiten der folgenden Jahre, von denen in diesem Quart-Band nur eine Auswahl vorgestellt wird. Das ihren Arbeiten zugrunde liegende Konzept konnten sie der Fachöffentlichkeit in mehreren Ausstellungen zur Diskussion stellen, beginnend 2011 in der Reihe *Formel_x* des Deutschen Architektur Zentrums (DAZ) in Berlin mit dem kryptischen Titel *In Love, to:*. Dem überraschten Publikum wurden dort nicht, wie bei Architekturausstellungen üblich, Pläne, Modelle und Dokumentarfotografien vorgestellt, sondern gezeigt wurde eine eigenwillige und subjektiv zusammengestellte Materialsammlung von Objekten, Zufallsfunden und Bildern unterschiedlichster Art, mit der AFF die Bildwelt andeuten wollten, die den Hintergrund ihrer Entwurfsarbeit darstellt. Selbstverständlich war dieser Einblick in die «Küche» des Büros keine Vorstellung von Rezepten, die sich 1:1 in den Projekten wiedererkennen liessen. Dazu ist eine solche Materialsammlung zu individuell und zufällig und andererseits der Entwurfsprozess von der Aufgabe her zu komplex und in Bezug auf die Zahl der Beteiligten zu dialogisch angelegt. Aber ihre Präsentation war dennoch bestens geeignet, auf den besonderen Umgang des Büros mit Fragen der Dauerhaftigkeit und Langlebigkeit von Formen, Bildern und Narrativen zu verweisen; auf ihr spezifisches Verständnis von der *firmitas*, von einer ästhetischen Nachhaltigkeit der Baukunst, die weit über die technischen Dimensionen hinausreicht, die so lange diskussionsbestimmend waren, aber auch über die allein auf Recycling und CO_2-Bilanzen fokussierten aktuellen Versuche einiger Entwurfsarchitekten, mit der ökologischen Debatte Schritt zu halten. Bei AFF kommt das lange Leben von Bildern und Formen bei ihrer Suche nach einer nachhaltigen Architektur als Ausdruck unserer Zeit wie von selbst wieder zu seinem Recht.

In Love, to:, Deutsches Architektur Zentrum (DAZ), Berlin, 2011
In Love, to:, Deutsches Architektur Zentrum (DAZ), Berlin, 2011

bricks that had often been developed and applied to many buildings in the GDR in cooperation with designers, sculptors and architects, and assembled these newly produced elements into a wall, which they inserted into their single-family home as a sense-giving element. In this way, they achieved a broader reference to the former history of the new neighbourhood than would have been possible by the more obvious gesture of picking up on the near by *Haus am Horn*, built in 1923, and the dogmas of the Bauhaus.

The handling of time and form, of material relics and idealistic concepts, that can be seen here is not a unique episode in the work of AFF and is anything but random. It points to a constitutive, perhaps even key aspect of their understanding of the sustainability and durability of building. When solving questions of design, it is aimed at harmonising their perception and memory with the construction and function of a building task, both conceptually and formally. This is evident in their works in subsequent years, of which this Quart book only presents a selection.

They were able to present the concept underlying their work to the specialist public for discussion in several exhibitions. The first of these was in 2011 in the series *Formel_x* by the Deutsches Architektur Zentrum DAZ in Berlin, with the cryptic title "In Love, to:". Instead of being shown plans, models and documentary photographs, as one might expect from an architectural exhibition, the surprised visitors were greeted by an extremely diverse, unconventional and subjectively compiled collection of objects, accidental finds and photos that hinted at the world of images that exists behind the architects' design work. Naturally, this view into the "kitchen" of their office was not a presentation of recipes that can be detected one-to-one in their projects. Such a collection of material is too individual and random for this, and on the other hand the design process is too complex in terms of its task and too dialogical in terms of the number of participants. But their presentation was nevertheless very well suited to refer to the special way that AFF handle questions concerning the durability and longevity of forms, images and narratives, as well as their particular understanding of *firmitas*: namely an aesthetic sustainability of architecture that reaches far beyond the technical dimensions that have defined discussion for so long, and far beyond current attempts by some architects to keep apace with ecological debate by focusing only on *recycling* and *carbon footprints*. The work of AFF ensures that the long life of images and forms naturally regains its rightful place in the search for sustainable architecture as an expression of our time.

SCHUTZHÜTTE, TELLERHÄUSER

MOUNTAIN HUT, TELLERHÄUSER

Die Schutzhütte liegt im Erzgebirge am Rande der Ortschaft Tellerhäuser und ersetzt einen Fertigteilbau aus den 1970er Jahren, der vor dem Leerstand als Skiservicestation genutzt wurde. Da auf dem Bauplatz nur geringfügige Erweiterungen zugelassen waren, kam ein Umbau nur unter Erhalt des desolaten Gebäudes in Betracht. So ummantelt die neue Fassade den Bestand, der als Schalung dient. Im Hauptraum der Hütte bleibt der vormalige Holzfertigteilbau als abstrakt-negativer Abdruck der kleinteiligen Struktur aus Holzlamellen, alten Sprossenfenstern und Tür präsent.

Von aussen zeigt sich die Hütte als minimalistisches Volumen. Abgeschottet zur Strasse, erkennt man die Zugänge nur anhand der Fugen der von Stahlrahmen gefassten Betontüren. Rückseitig geben fünf verzinkte grossflächige Stahlrahmenfenster den Blick auf die Gebirgsvegetation frei. Akzentuiert wird der eingeschossige Baukörper an einer Schmalseite durch ein kaminartiges Oberlicht. Hier befindet sich im offenen Raumkontinuum ein asketischer Rückzugsort.

Schlicht in technischer sowie funktionaler Hinsicht, erfüllt der Bau seinen Zweck als spartanische Schutzhütte: mit einem schützenden Dach, zwei Feuerstellen zum Heizen und Kochen, einem Essplatz und einer Aufenthaltszone. An den kalten Schmalseiten befinden sich, blickgeschützt hinter raumhohen Wandscheiben, die Schlafplätze. Das ergänzte Volumen unter dem ehemaligen Vordach bildet eine Pufferzone zur Strasse aus, in der dienende Funktionen untergebracht sind, wie Waschraum, Toilette und ein von aussen zugängliches Ski- und Gerätelager. Die Ausstattung besteht aus wiederverwendeten Bauteilen wie alten Stahlöfen, Waschbecken, Lampen und Möbeln.

The project is situated in the Ore Mountains on the outskirts of the village and replaces a prefabricated timber building from the 1970s, which had been used as a service station by a ski sports club before becoming redundant. Since only a limited amount of the land around the building site can be used together with the existing structure, including a small extension, it was only feasible to convert it while preserving what remained of the building, which was in a dilapidated condition. Thus, the new façade envelopes the existing building, acting as formwork around it. In this way, it was not only possible to create additional space for the auxiliary rooms beneath the space of the former canopy, but it also opened up the hidden view of the building interior. The dialectic texture defines the main room of the cabin, consisting of a small-scale structure of wooden slats, old muntin windows and doors.

From the outside, the building presents itself as a minimalist concrete volume. Shielded from the street, one can only recognise the entrances due to the joints of the steel frames for the concrete doors. On the forest side, five galvanised steel-framed windows compose a panorama of the mountain vegetation along the entire width of the building. The single-storey structure is accentuated on a narrow side by a chimney-like, ascending skylight. The building is now an ascetic retreat with an open spatial continuum.

With its consistently minimalist intent, the building fulfils its purpose as a Spartan shelter, both technologically and regarding its function: with a protective roof, two fireplaces for heating and cooking, a dining area and a living zone. The bedroom areas are situated at the cold head end, visually shielded by room-high shear walls. The added volume beneath the canopy of the old building is regarded as a buffer zone towards the road. It accommodates auxiliary rooms such as a laundry, a toilet and a niche for a frost-secure water supply, as well as a ski and equipment store, which can be accessed from outside. The cabin was conceived with fittings made of recycled building elements, such as steel stoves, lamps, washbasins and light switches.

Planung und Ausführung: 2007–2010
Planning and construction: 2007–2010

Fertigteil-Bungalow, Typ «Weißwasser» (DDR-Werbebroschüre)
Prefabricated bungalow element, "Weisswasser" type (GDR advertising brochure)

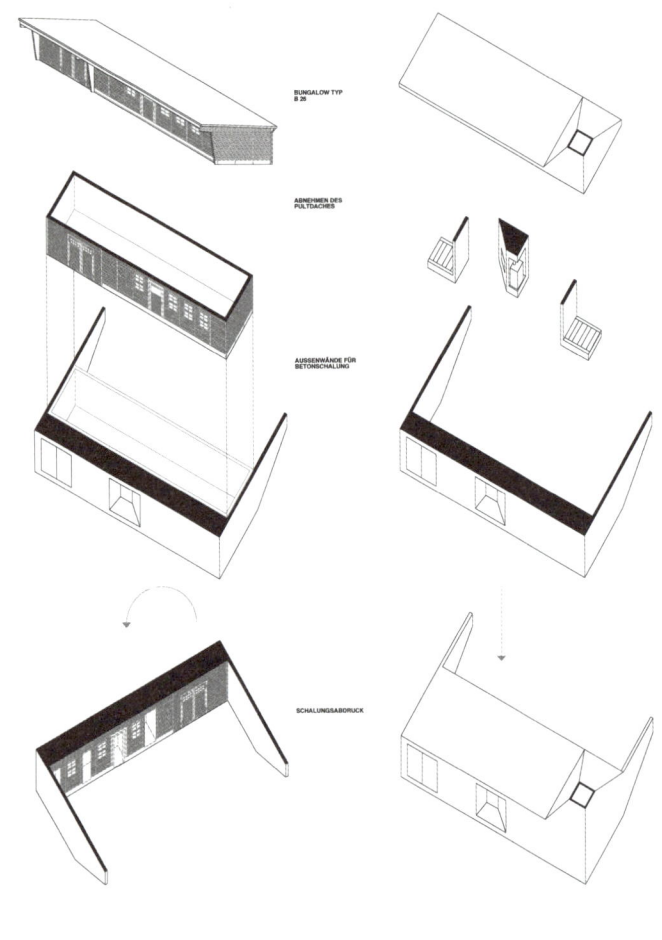

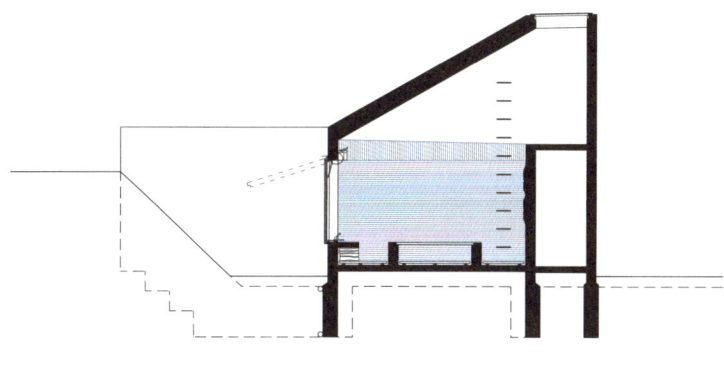

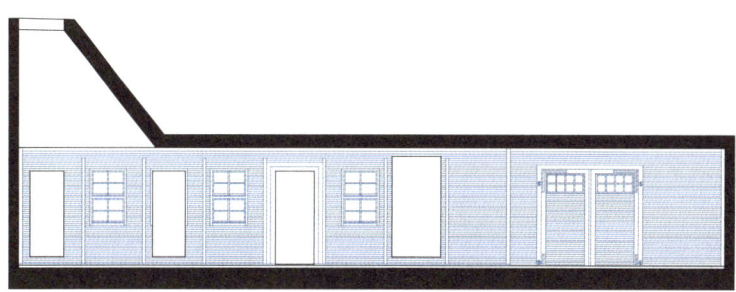
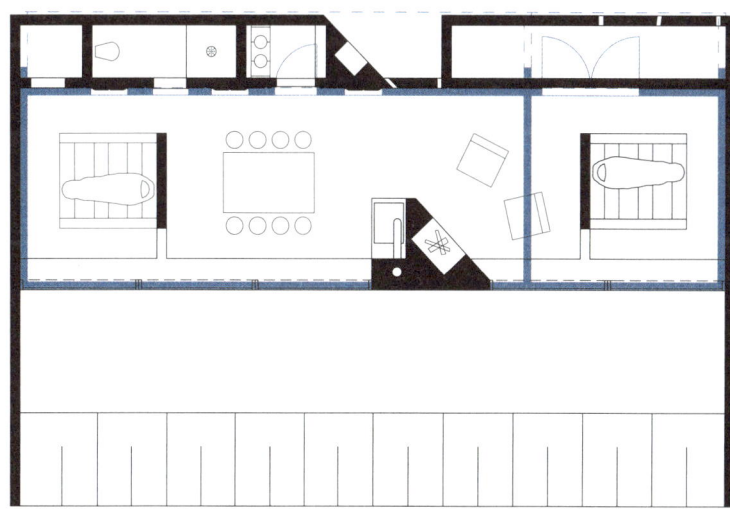

LINDETAL HOUSE, MECKLENBURG-WEST POMERANIA

The residential building was constructed in Mecklenburg in a village type known as an *Angerdorf*.[1] It was produced as the result of an obsession to construct something that appreciated the value of construction and respected the traditionally itinerant carpenter's trade. The demanding, precisely fitting, metal-free joints form the heart of the construction. Their materially compatible thrust joints represent an autonomous thesis on sustainable building.

The project focuses on the craft's production process by questioning the material logistics of today's construction methods. The project is an antithesis of the logic of manufactured products, so all working processes were produced on location without additional transport requirements, using the know-how available at the building site. For the duration of the building process, a provisional building cabin was erected that served both as accommodation and as a workshop. A local cross-cutting and trenching site was combined with a timber store to supplement the ensemble of the temporary production site. This allowed 55 m³ of Douglas fir, oak, larch and ash timber that was cut in the winter to be processed as a local resource.

The building is supported by a concrete base that is internally structured into two separate living areas by means of wall and staircase elements. On this monolithic sculpture, four main oak frames stand upon an oak outlining frame, their bracing diagonal bows remaining visible in the living area. The load-bearing structure is a pinewood frame, while the beams are carefully joined using traditional carpenter's methods, using offsetting, pins and trunnels. The exterior envelope is dominated by seamless, waney-edged larch wood boards.

The interior spatial organisation assumes the typology of a traditional "low German house". It was historically widespread from Amsterdam to Gdansk. During agrarian times, it stood for living with one's livestock under a single roof. A central vestibule, which was more like a hall and therefore gave the type its German name "Hallenhaus", accommodated the fireplace and also acted as a distributor to all adjoining spaces for people and livestock. In the Lindetal House, it was converted into a living hall with an adjoining kitchen, warehouse and bedrooms. The generous glazing towards the garden adds an impressive panorama of the landscape over the gentle slope.

[1] An *Angerdorf* is built either side of an elongated village green.

In collaboration with Stephan Hahn, architect and carpenter
Planning and construction: 2014–2016

"Groot Dääl" in a 19th-century four-framed house
The rural architecture of the "low German house" once characterised the region from Amsterdam to Gdansk (image: Wandland Archiv)

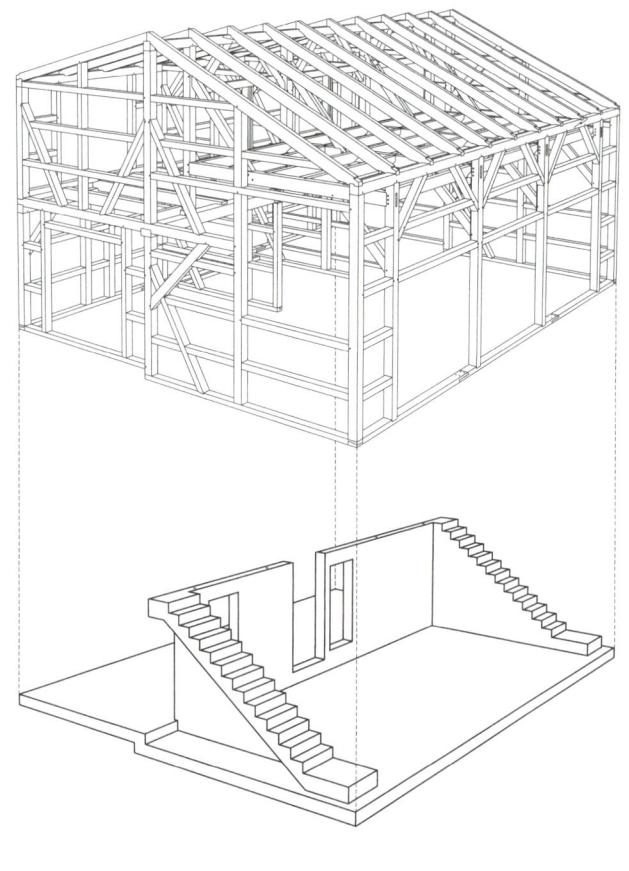

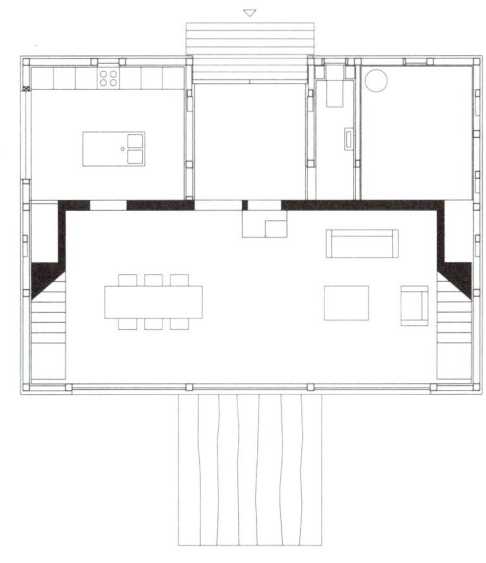
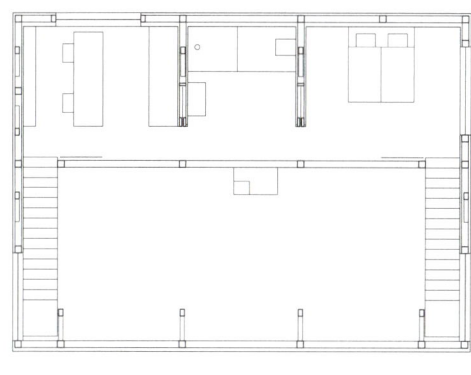
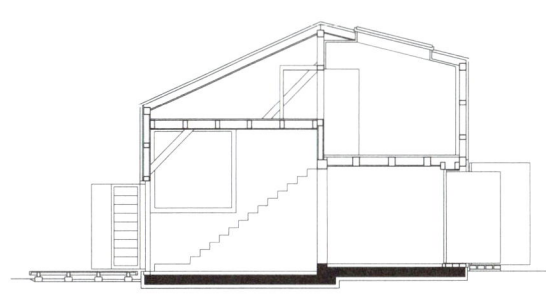
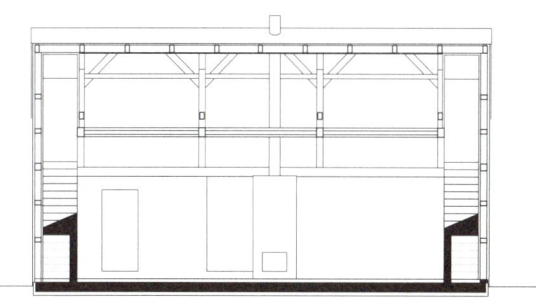

WOHNBLOCK ELF FREUNDE, BERLIN

"ELF FREUNDE" HOUSING BLOCK, BERLIN

Der Wohnblock wurde auf der letzten unbebauten Parzelle des urbanen Flickenteppichs eines 130 Hektar grossen Areals am Rummelsburger See errichtet. Hierbei handelt es sich um ein ehemaliges Industriegebiet, das zu einer Wohnnutzung umgestaltet wurde.

Der Gebäuderiegel vereint elf schmale viergeschossige Stadthäuser in sich und zielt auf eine dichte Nachbarschaft. Trotz der gestalterischen Strenge der städtebaulichen Grossform liegt der Fokus auf den individuellen Gestaltungsmöglichkeiten der inneren Räume durch die Bewohnerschaft. Die Varianz der individuellen Aufteilung des immer gleichen Raumvolumens spiegelt die generelle Vielfalt städtischen Wohnens wider. Sie reicht von der konventionellen Kleinteiligkeit mehrerer Räume pro Etage über durchgesteckte Räume je Geschoss bis zu geschossübergreifenden Räumen. Innerhalb eines definierten Rasters gab es verschiedene Möglichkeiten, individuelle Deckenöffnungen sowie Raum- und Terrassengrössen zu wählen. Lediglich die Lage der inneren Treppen an einer der Trennwände wurde als verbindlich vorgegeben, entweder als Kaskade oder mit einzelnen Treppenläufen. Damit reflektiert das Projekt eine intensive Beschäftigung mit dem klassischen Reihenhaustyp, der in der Regel eine Wiederholung des gleichen Moduls darstellt. Doch im Unterschied dazu wurde der Wohnblock aus einem Baukastenprinzip von Elementen entwickelt, die eine reiche Kombinatorik an Möglichkeiten bieten.

Die Unterteilung der einzelnen Privathäuser wird an der Nordfassade durch unterschiedliche Texturen in den Putzflächen ablesbar. Im Kontrast dazu erscheint die Südfassade als einheitliche Front im Wechselspiel eingeschnittener Terrassen und grosser Fensterelemente. Zugunsten kleiner Vorgärten an der Eingangsseite, die als Spiel- und Begegnungszone genutzt werden, sind die Stellplätze gemeinschaftlich in einem offenen Carport an den Schmalseiten des Wohnblocks angeordnet.

The housing block was placed on the last undeveloped plot of the urban patchwork of a 130-hectare area by the Rummelsburger See. This is a development zone that was mainly used for industrial purposes in former times and is now being transformed into a residential landscape with commercial areas and green spaces.

The rectangular structure unites 11 narrow four-storey townhouses and is aimed at close neighbourly relationships. Despite the stringent design of the overall urban-planning development, the focus lies on the residents' individual design potential for the interior spaces. Variations in the individual partitioning of the always identical spatial volume reflects the general diversity of urban living. It ranges from several conventional small-scale rooms on a single floor to continuous rooms on one floor and even multi-level areas. Within a defined grid, there are various available possibilities, including individual ceiling apertures and room and terrace sizes. Only the location of the interior stairs along one of the partition walls is binding, either as a cascade or with individual flights. The project thereby reflects the intensive engagement with the classic type of terraced housing, which generally repeats the same module. By contrast however, the "Elf Freunde" housing block consists of a modular principle of elements that enable a wide variety of combinations.

The development's subdivision into individual private homes becomes clearly legible on the northern façade, with different textures in the plaster surfaces and individual entrances. The south façade is different, presenting a uniform front with an interplay of incised terraces and large window elements made of bronze-anodised aluminium. The parking spaces are located in open garages on the narrow side of the housing block, enabling small forecourt gardens that are used as playing areas and meeting zones.

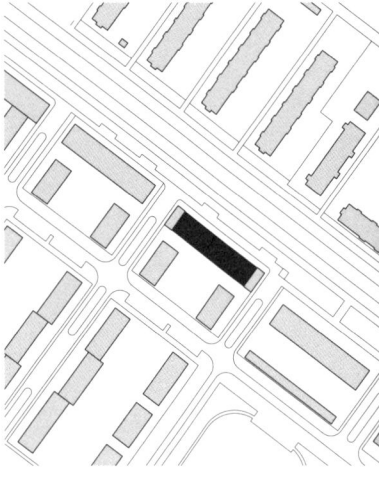

Planung und Ausführung: 2010–2012
Planning and construction: 2010–2012

Kinderreiche Familie, 1930 (Bild: Bundesarchiv, Berlin)
Family with many children, 1930 (image: Bundesarchiv, Berlin)

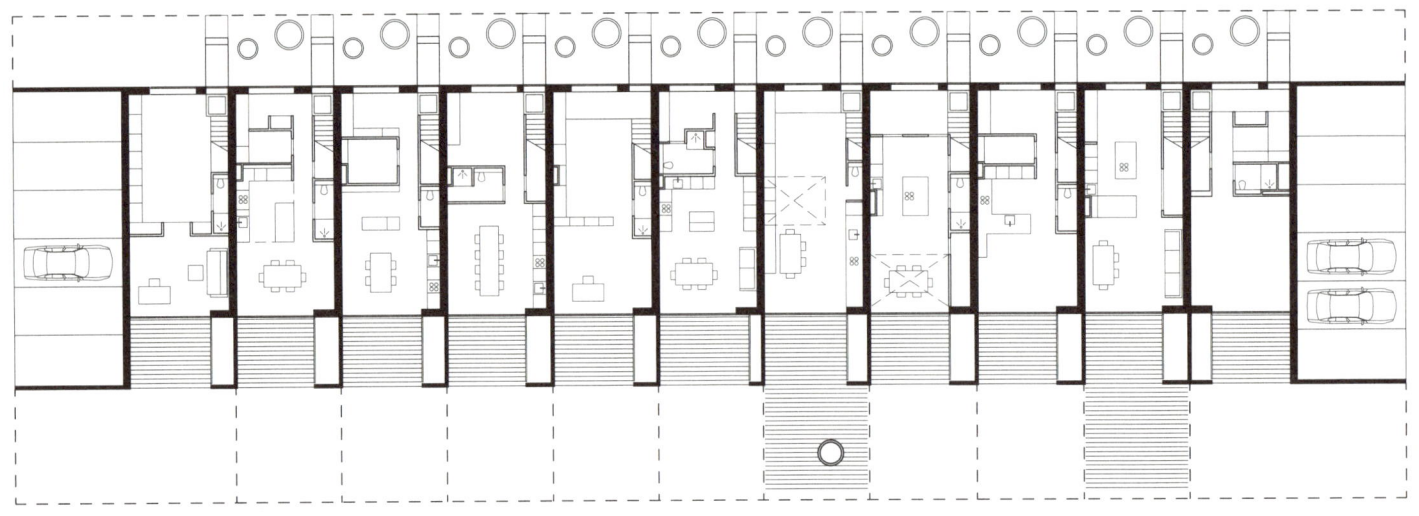

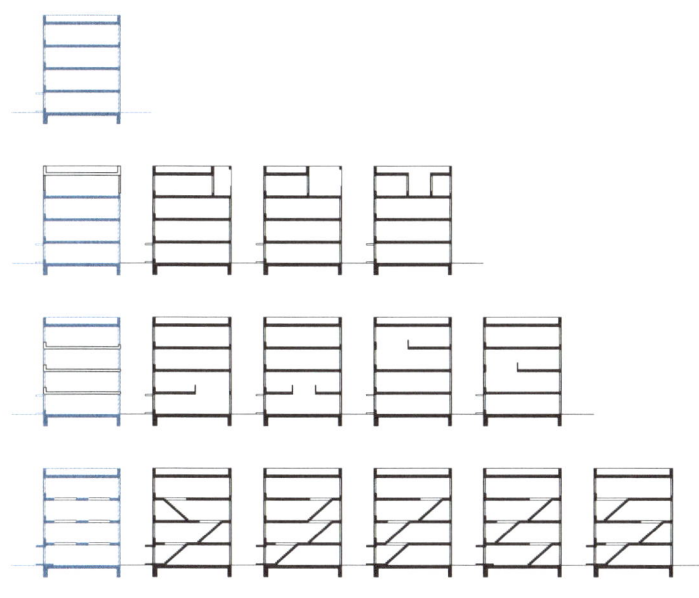

TAUFZENTRUM KIRCHE ST. PETRI-PAULI, LUTHERSTADT EISLEBEN

CHRISTENING CENTRE, ST. PETRI-PAULI CHURCH, EISLEBEN

Die Kirche St. Petri-Pauli befindet sich in der Lutherstadt Eisleben, die heute noch von den Spuren der Reformationszeit geprägt ist. Sie wird, wie eine Vielzahl von Gebäuden der Stadt, in der Liste der Weltkulturstätten geführt.

Das Projekt verfolgt das Ziel, die dreischiffige spätgotische Hallenkirche in ein Taufzentrum mit übergemeindlicher und überkonfessioneller Ausstrahlung umzugestalten. Dabei stehen die Überlegungen zur Neugestaltung und Neugewichtung des Gotteshauses im Spannungsfeld zwischen der Bedeutung der originalen Stätte als Taufkirche Martin Luthers und dem Anspruch der Kirche, zeitgemäss und offen zu sein.

Der Eingriff in den gewachsenen Ort beschränkt sich auf den Kirchenboden, in den das neue Taufbecken für Immersionstaufen an der Schnittstelle von Kirchenhalle und Chorraum integriert wird. Hier öffnet sich die Bodenplatte kreisrund und hält einen leichten Abstand zur fliessenden Wasseroberfläche des darunter befindlichen Beckens. Mit einer umlaufenden Fuge setzt sich der neue Betonboden von der denkmalgeschützten Substanz ab. Die Gravur in seiner Oberfläche referiert auf Interferenzen einer Wasseroberfläche. Zum einen gehen diese Ringe vom Taufbecken und der Lutherrose aus, zum anderen laufen sie von den räumlichen Polen ausgehend nach innen und überlagern sich. Der neue Boden fliesst nach aussen zum Kirchenvorplatz mit einer geneigten Rampe zum schwellenfreien Eintritt.

Der neue Sockel des spätgotischen Annenaltars entwickelt sich wie das Taufbecken aus dem Betonboden, er ist Hauptaltar und nicht mehr vom Kirchenschiff durch eine Schwelle getrennt. Ergänzt wird das Ensemble durch einen weiteren, mobilen Altar und andere Prinzipalen. Das Kirchengestühl sowie alle neuen Ausstattungen sind konsequent aus verschiedenen regionalen Obsthölzern handwerklich gefertigt.

The St. Petri-Pauli Church is situated in Lutherstadt Eisleben, which is still characterised by traces of the Reformation period today. Like many of the buildings in the town, it is listed as World Cultural Heritage.

The project is aimed at converting the three-winged late-Gothic hall church into a christening centre with a multi-congregational and non-denominational expression. In this respect, considerations to redesign and newly assign the house of God had to weigh up the importance of the original site as the church where Martin Luther was christened and the church's ambition to be contemporary and open.

The measure to the organically developed location is limited to the church floor, into which the new baptismal font for immersive christenings is integrated at the threshold between the church hall and the choir. The floor plates open up in a circular form, maintaining a slight distance from the flowing water surface of the basin beneath it.

A surrounding joint sets the new concrete floor apart from the preservation-listed building substance. Its engravings refer to ripples on water surfaces. On the one hand, these rings emanate from the baptismal font and the Luther rose, while on the other, they run inwards from spatial poles and overlap. The new floor flows outwards onto the church forecourt with a ramp that is suitable for barrier-free access.

The new base of the late Gothic Annenaltar develops out of the floor like the baptismal font. It is the main altar and is no longer separated from the nave by a threshold. The ensemble is supplemented by an additional mobile altar and other principals. Like the church seating, all new furnishing is consistently made by carpenters using various regional types of wood from orchard trees.

In Zusammenarbeit mit Georgi Architektur und Stadtplanung
Planung und Ausführung: 2011–2012
Wettbewerb 2010

In collaboration with Georgi Architektur und Stadtplanung
Planning and construction: 2011–2012
Competition: 2010

Lutherstadt Eisleben und Mansfelder Land
Eisleben and the Mansfelder Land region

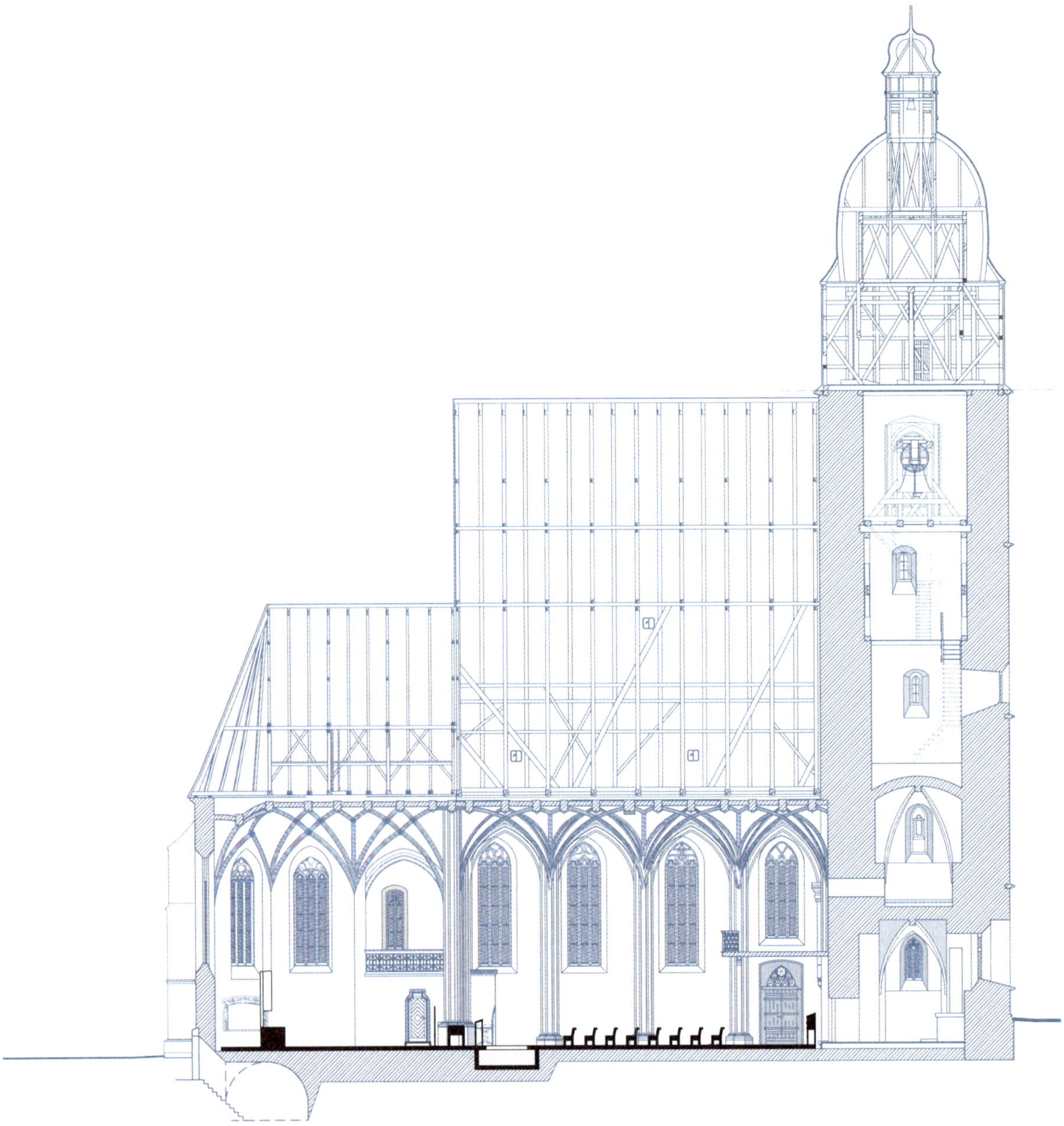

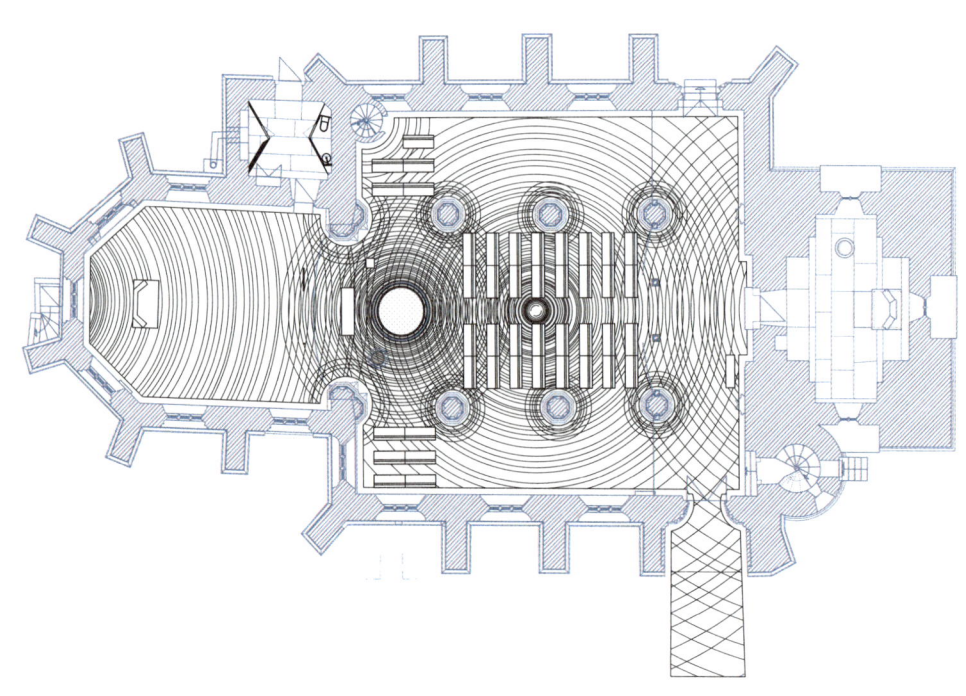

34

CONVERSION OF THE MAIN FREIGHT RAILWAY STATION, HANOVER

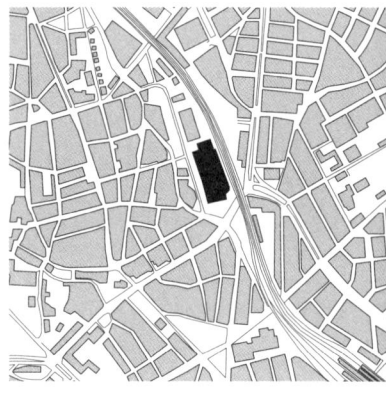

Planung und Ausführung: 2013–2019
Planning and construction: 2013–2019

The expansive hall complex defines an inner-urban development zone between railway tracks, heterogeneous residential neighbourhoods and Continental AG factories. The complex was built in 1930 as the main freight hall for the line between Hanover and Hamburg/Bremen. At the time, it was the largest and most modern railway logistics facility in Europe. In the 1950s, it was expanded to cover an area of 40,000 m^2 and served as the central goods reloading location for the greater Hanover region. The location gradually lost its significance as freight transport began to use other means. Due to its vacancy since 1997, the hall building fell into decay for almost 20 years.

The project sounds out the potential of the balancing act of converting industrial logistics structures into urban leisure facilities by attempting to translate the qualities of the open hall typology into appropriate use scenarios, while also achieving a neighbourly dialogue with the surrounding urban landscape using appropriate parks and open spaces. Thus the concept initially envisages roughly halving the hall's area to 22,000 m^2, with the aim of creating a shell for flexible uses and large leisure areas for activities needing high ceilings, such as trampolining, boulder climbing and fitness exercises, which are complemented by a wide range of gastronomic services. The internal mobility axis affords a view of the steel girders with their regular rhythm of rivets, reminding users of the architecture's industrial past and recalling the 1930s.

Like a carpet, the plan for the open spaces developed by Topotek1 interweaves the indoor and outdoor areas to create a large, fluent space. The dark grey asphalt surrounding the hall is covered with a white zebra pattern, which characterises the large forecourt and the new urban terrace, as well as continuing into the publicly accessible areas inside the hall.

Hauptgüterbahnhof um 1970
Main freight railway station around 1970

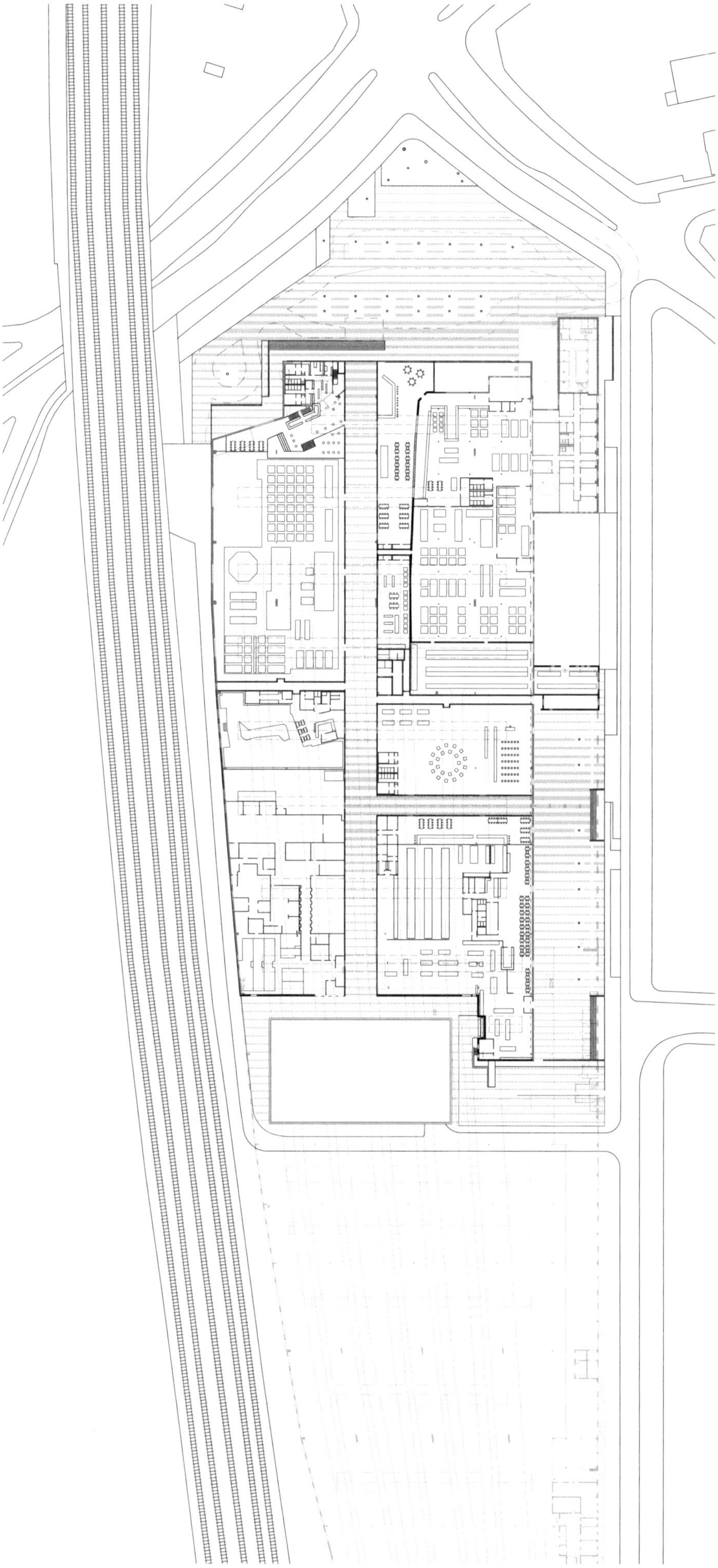

43

URBAN WORKSHOP, BERLIN

The aim of Berlin's Senate Administration and Urban Planning Office is urban development with civic participation in the heart of Berlin. An address was sought for this new platform. The "Stadtwerkstatt" or "Urban Workshop" is situated on the 1st floor of a 13-storey prefabricated housing block from the 1960s and is accessed via a public walkway. It was once part of the prestigious centre of East Berlin, opposite the TV tower and the Town Hall known as the "Rote Rathaus". Today, it is surrounded by shops, fast-food chains and a fluctuating array of commercial enterprises and has itself been the subject of conversions and structural adaptation.

The current intervention aimed to focus on sustainability in handling material resources, rather than demolition and the installation of fake surfaces. Thus the concept picks up on the morbid, sober charm of the former office floor and initially pools what can be used from among the existing fabric. The reinforced concrete structure was therefore partially exposed down to the shell construction, while obsolete installations were removed. The demonstratively large opening in the grid ceiling provided material for other dilapidated areas and now defines a centre in the public space. Its unadorned appearance provides insight into the constructive rawness of the existing structure. An integrated kitchen invites visitors to stay and eat, while a curtain made of scaffolding gauze visually partitions the room. The information and warehouse counter made out of recycled shopping trolleys was developed by the designer Ilja Oelschlägel.

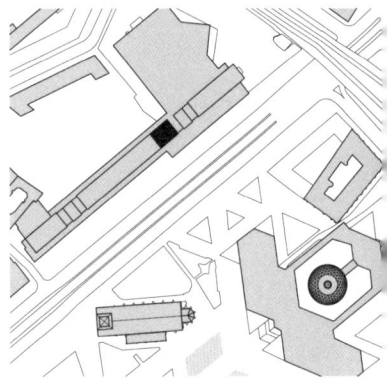

Planning and construction: 2017–2018

Karl-Liebknecht-Strasse with special Type-P2 buildings, 1982 (image: Bundesarchiv, Berlin)

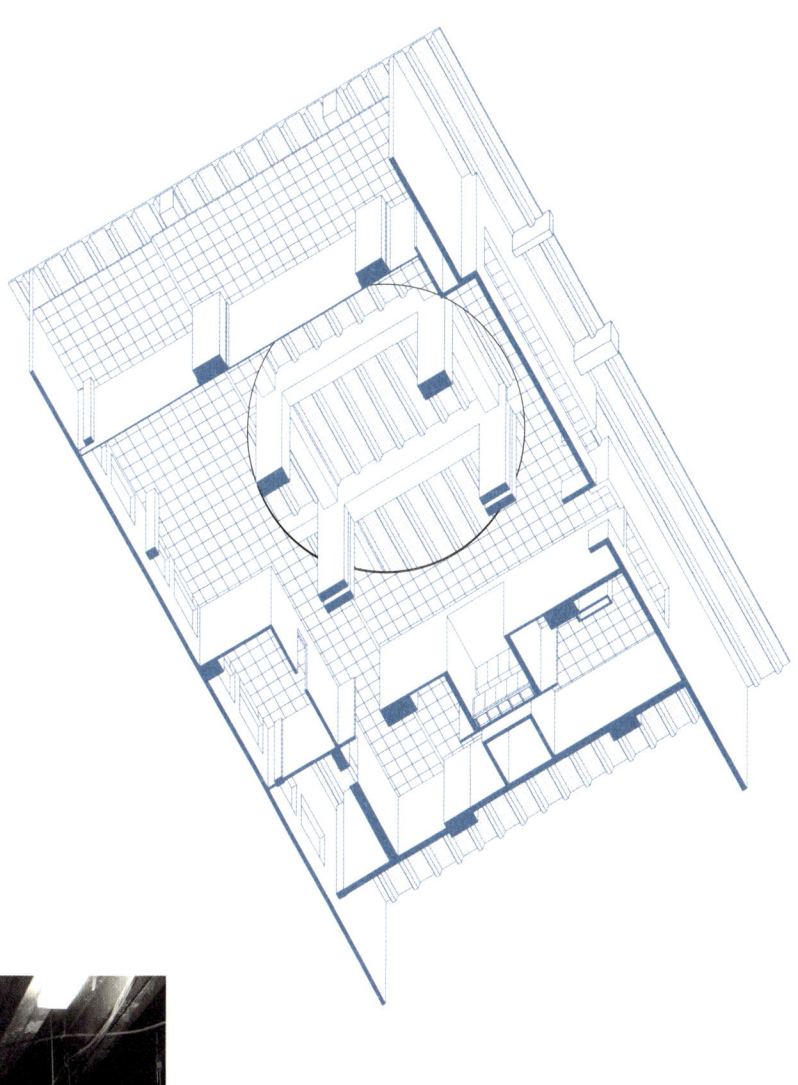

SÄCHSISCHE LANDESAUSSTELLUNG, ZWICKAU

SAXON STATE EXHIBITION, ZWICKAU

Sachsen ist eine Wiege der deutschen Industrialisierung. Entsprechend naheliegend war der Entschluss, die Leitausstellung zur 500-jährigen Industriekulturgeschichte im Rahmen der 4. Sächsischen Landesaustellung in der Audi-Halle in Zwickau zu präsentieren. Der von Theophil Quaysin für die Auto Union AG 1938/39 erbaute Bestandsbau wurde seinerzeit unter der Massgabe der grösstmöglichen Einsparung und dem Ziel einer möglichst eisenarmen Bauweise errichtet.

Die heutigen Eingriffe und Sanierungsarbeiten wurden nach der gleichen Massgabe konzipiert und unterstreichen den ursprünglichen Charakter des Gebäudes. Für die An- und Neubauten wurde ein Konzept gesucht, welches nicht nur auf die technischen Anforderungen der hohen Besucherströme eingeht, sondern auch zu Fragen der Nachhaltigkeit und temporären Nutzungen in unserer Zeit Stellung bezieht. Das umgesetzte Gestaltkonzept geht darüber hinaus: Es nutzt repetitiv vorhandene Massenprodukte und kombiniert sie zu neuen dienenden Bauteilen. Ein zweigeschossiges Eingangsgebäude zum Empfang der Besucherinnen und Besucher und eine Rampenanlage als behindertengerechter Ausstellungszugang in die ehemalige Montage- und Produktionshalle wurden demontierbar aus Seecontainern entworfen. Das Öffnen und Schliessen der weiten Eingangshalle wird mit einer ausladenden Geste eines 6 Meter hohen Vorhanges zelebriert. Die Entwicklung der Ausstattungselemente, wie Tresen und Schliessfächer aus Werkzeugkisten, sowie Sitzmöbeln aus Autoreifen, folgt konsequent dem Leitbild der Nachnutzung. Themen wie industrielles Erbe, Produktaustausch und Recyclingprozesse werden somit als gestaltbestimmende Ästhetik lesbar. In Zusammenarbeit mit dem Designer Ilja Oelschlägel entstanden Objekte aus bekannten Elementen, wobei jedes Objekt seinen eigenen prägenden Charakter entwickelt, indem es die erste Nutzung nicht verleugnet.

Saxony is the cradle of German industrialisation. Thus, it was logical to decide to present a leading exhibition on its 500-year industrial history at the 4th Saxon State Exhibition in the Audi Hall, Zwickau. The existing structure, which was built by Theophil Quaysin for Auto Union AG in 1938–1939, was erected on the principle of maximum possible savings and the aim of building methods using as little iron as possible.

Today's measures and renovation work were conceived according to the same principles and respected the original character of the building. The new and extension buildings required a concept that not only engages with the technical demands of the considerable visitor flows, but also declares a stance on questions of sustainability in our times. The implemented design concept goes even further. It uses repeatedly existent mass-produced items and combines them to form newly usable building elements. A two-storey entrance building with a ramp facility to receive exhibition visitors in the former assembly and production site was designed out of shipping containers that can later be dismantled. The opening and closing of the broad entrance hall is celebrated with the sweeping gesture of a 6-metre high curtain. The development of the fitted elements, such as counters and lockers made of toolboxes, as well as seating furniture made of car tyres, consistently applies the principle of reuse. Themes such as industrial heritage, product exchange and recycling processes are thereby made legible as aesthetic elements that define the design. In collaboration with the designer Ilja Oelschlägel, objects were produced out of well-known elements, whereby each object develops its own definitive character by negating its original use.

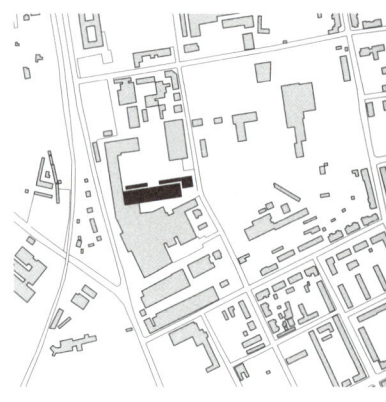

In Zusammenarbeit mit Georgi Architektur und Stadtplanung
Wettbewerb 2017
Planung und Ausführung: 2018–2020

In collaboration with Georgi Architektur und Stadtplanung
Competition: 2017
Planning and construction: 2018–2020

Montagehalle der AUTO UNION AG, um 1938 (Bild: Archiv August Horch Museum, Zwickau)

AUTO UNION AG around 1938 (image: Archiv August Horch Museum Zwickau)

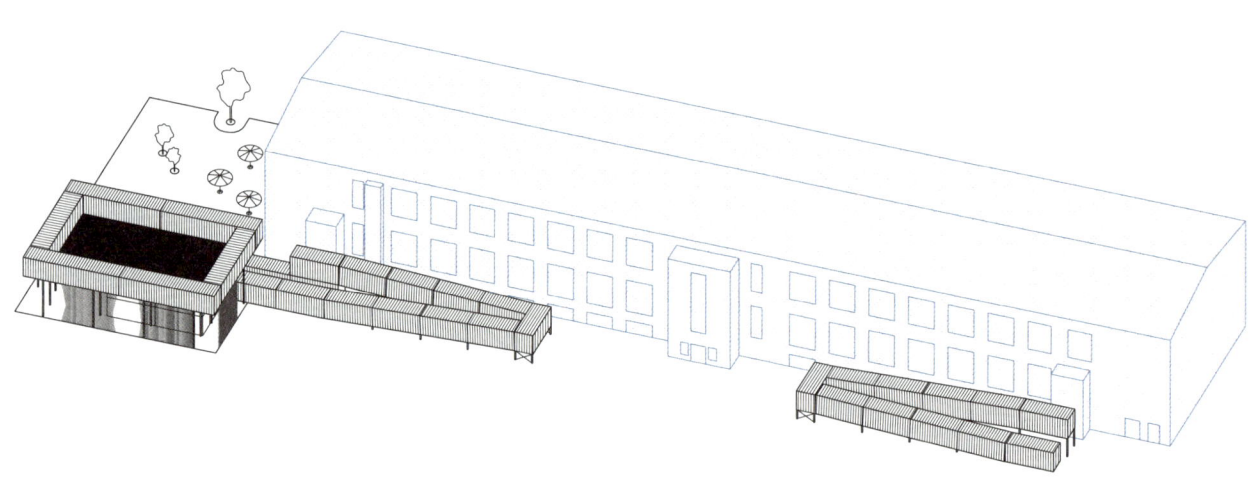

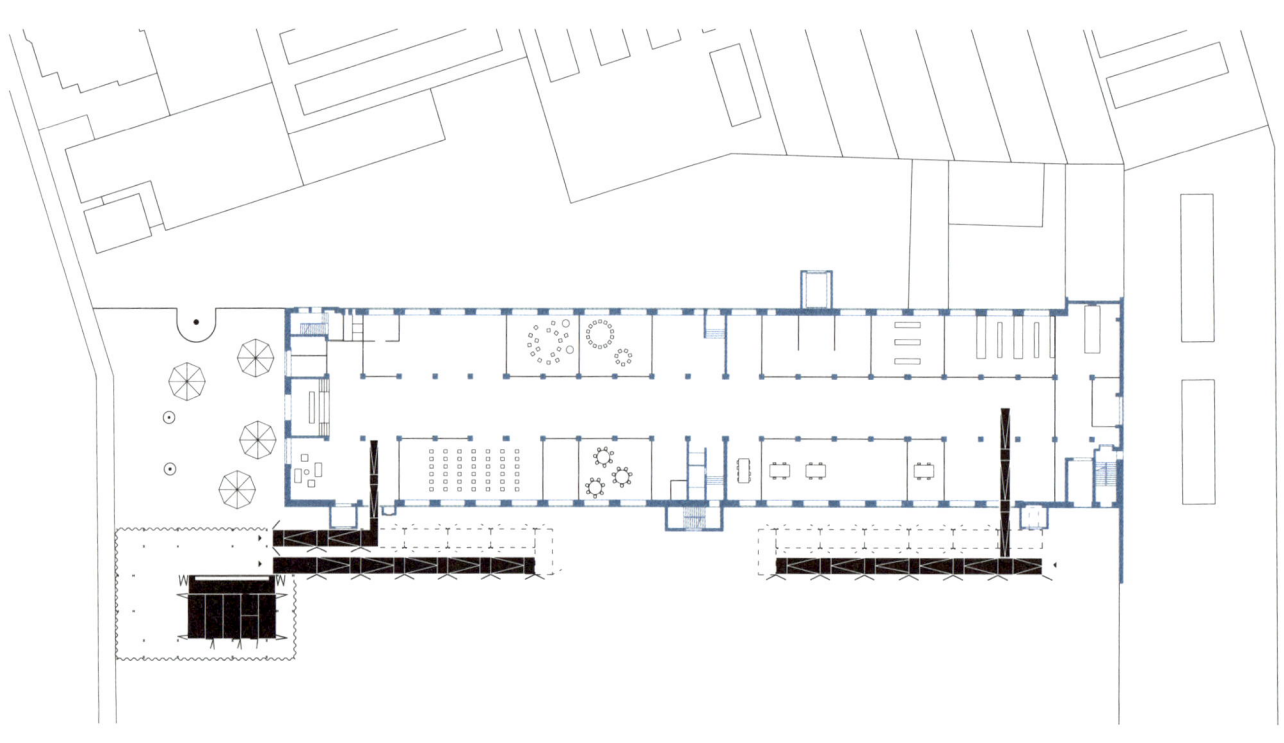

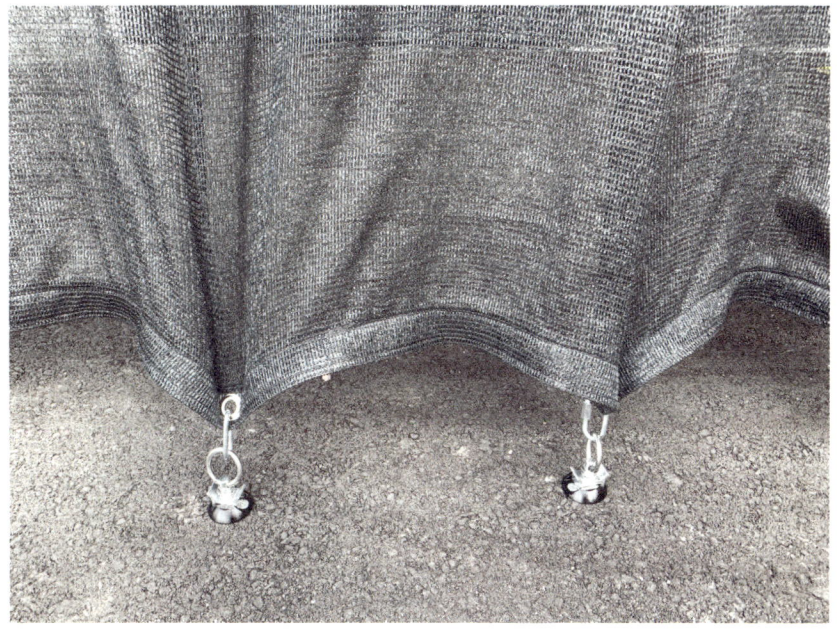

SPORE INITIATIVE, BERLIN

Das Projekt an der Hermannstraße in Berlin-Neukölln positioniert sich zu zwei unterschiedlichen urbanen Parametern. Einerseits markiert es die Grenze zum historischen Friedhof der Jerusalem Gemeinde und anderseits integriert es einen denkmalgeschützten Anflugbefeuerungsmast des naheliegenden Flughafens Tempelhof. Aus diesen Gegebenheiten resultiert ein Baukörper für die gemeinnützige Spore Initiative, der Raumabfolgen wie ein offenes Forum im Erdgeschoss, geschützte Ausstellungs- und Projekträume sowie Ateliers und eine offene Dachterrasse im Obergeschoss verknüpft. Die Spore Initiative versteht sich als ein kultureller Raum für multidisziplinäres Zusammenarbeiten, Experimentieren und Lernen. Ihre Projekte und Aktivitäten werden in engem Austausch mit lokal organisierten Initiativen auf der ganzen Welt entwickelt, die sich der Regeneration der Biosphäre und dem Widerstand gegen und der Bekämpfung von Umweltungerechtigkeiten widmen. Dazu organisiert und veranstaltet Spore eine Vielzahl unterschiedlicher Formate und Aktivitäten in Berlin und weltweit.

In Tradition der Berliner Klinkerarchitektur sowie der Trümmerverwertung nach dem Zweiten Weltkrieg wird die Fassade von wiederverwendeten Backsteinen bestimmt. Im Inneren setzt sich der Ansatz des Bauteilrecyclings in differierenden Elementen fort. Die Decke des Forums referiert auf Studien zum realen Kraftfluss. Ihre Unterzüge werden aus den Hauptspannungstrajektorien entwickelt und optimieren somit den Materialeinsatz.

The project at Hermannstrasse in Berlin-Neukölln faces two different urban parameters. Firstly, it marks the boundary of the historical Jerusalem congregation cemetery. Secondly, it integrates a preservation-listed approach-lighting mast from the nearby former Tempelhof airport. These conditions have resulted in a building for the Spore Initiative, a registered charity that combines spatial sequences like an open forum on the ground floor, as well as protected exhibition and project rooms, studios and an open rooftop terrace on the upper level. The Spore Initiative regards itself as a cultural space for multidisciplinary collaboration, experimentation and learning. Its projects and activities are developed in close exchange with locally organised initiatives all around the world that are dedicated to biosphere regeneration and the struggle against environmental injustice. Furthermore, Spore arranges a large number of different formats and activities in Berlin and worldwide.

In the tradition of Berlin brickwork architecture and the reuse of war-induced rubble following World War II, the façades are defined by reused bricks. Inside, the principle of recycled building elements is continued in differentiating elements. The forum ceiling refers to studies on the real flux of forces. Its joists are developed from the main tension trajectories, thereby optimising the use of materials.

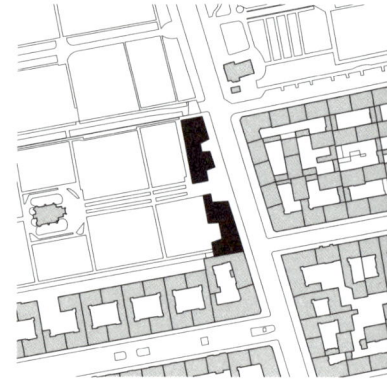

Wettbewerb: 2018
Planung und Ausführung: 2018–2021

**Competition: 2018
Planning and construction: 2018–2021**

Anflugbefeuerung für den ehemaligen Flughafen Tempelhof, Berlin (Bild: Stefan Rettich)

Approach lighting for the former Tempelhof Airport (image: Stefan Rettich)

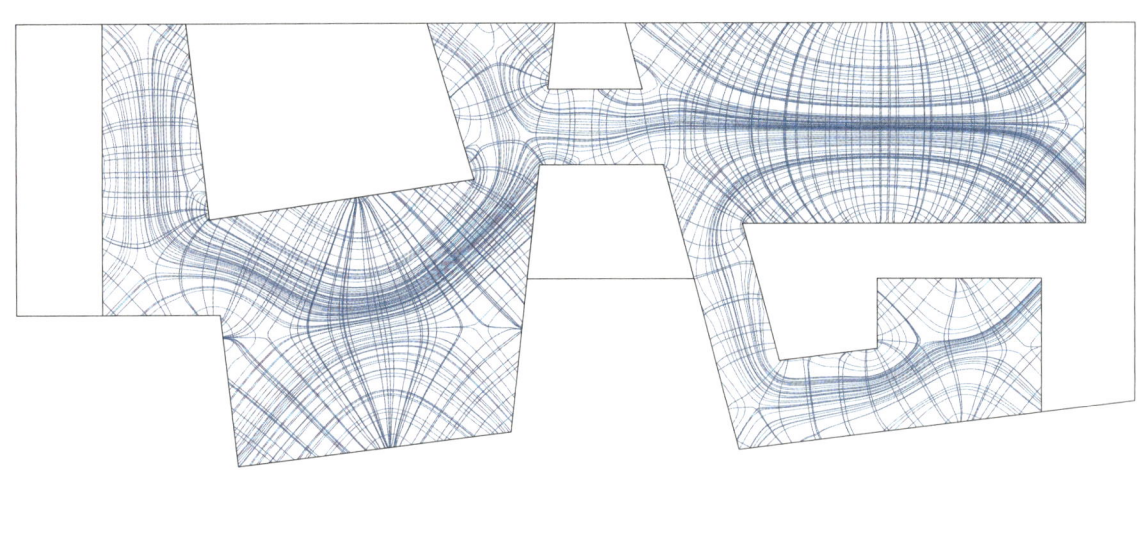

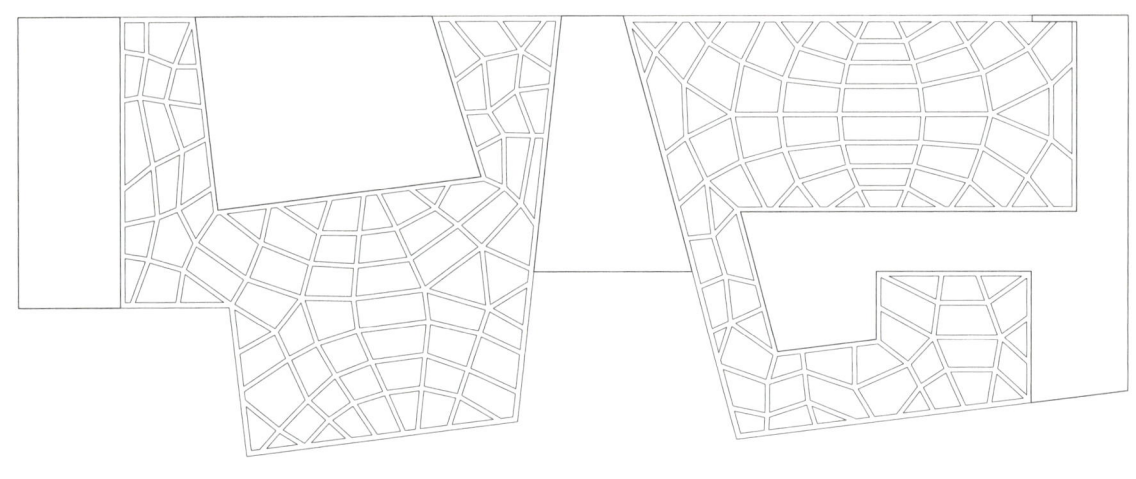

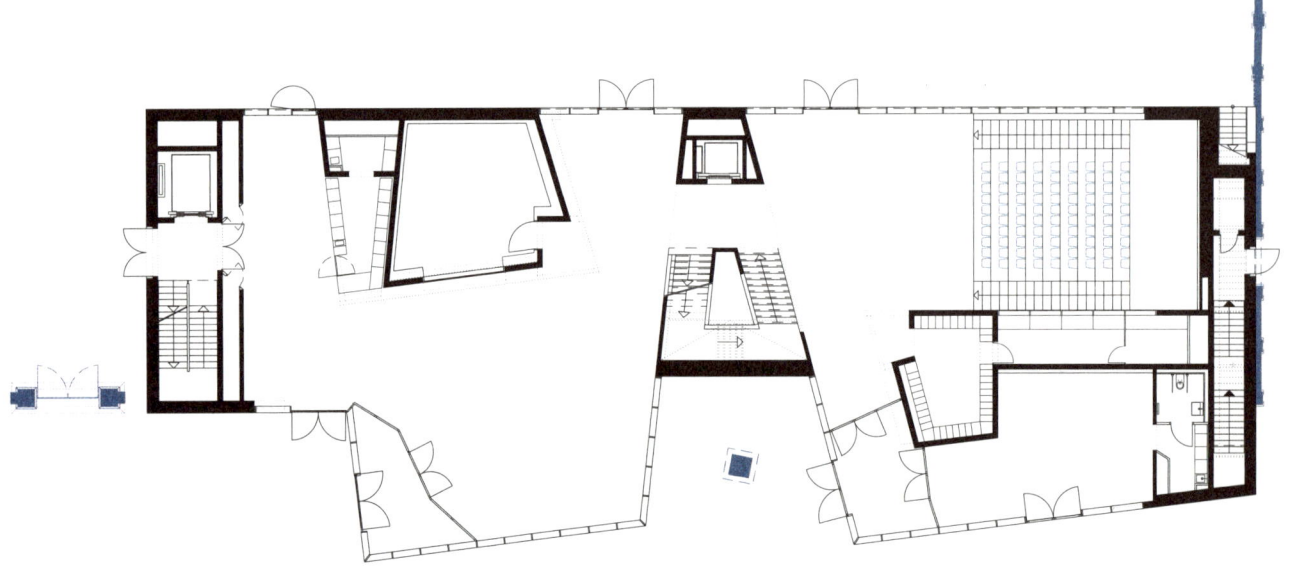

WERKVERZEICHNIS
Auswahl Bauten, Projekte und Wettbewerbe

2000	1	Sequenz, temporärer Arbeitsraum, Weimar
2006	2	Wohnhaus Zivcec, Weimar
2008	3	Umbau Schloss Freudenstein, Freiberg
		Terra Mineralia, TU Bergakademie, Freiberg
2010	4	Gemeinschaftsschule Anna Seghers, Berlin
		Schutzhütte, Tellerhäuser
		Wettbewerb Foyer Kunst- und Ausstellungshalle der BRD, Bonn (1. Preis)
		Wettbewerb Probebühnenzentrum Deutsches Theater, Berlin (2. Preis)
		Wettbewerb Erweiterung Sprengel-Museum, Hannover (4. Preis)
2011	5	*In Love, to:*, Deutsches Architektur Zentrum (DAZ), Berlin
	6	Lokschuppen Wriezener Bahnhof, Berlin
		Wettbewerb Gedenkstätte Ahlem, Hannover (2. Preis)
2012		Ludwig-Hoffmann-Grundschule, Berlin
		Taufzentrum St. Petri-Pauli, Lutherstadt Eisleben
		Wettbewerb Archäologisches Besucherzentrum am Petriplatz, Berlin (2. Preis)
		Wettbewerb Erweiterung Jüdisches Museum, Frankfurt a.M. (Anerkennung)
2012		*Luftfahrt*, Verkehrsmuseum, Dresden
2013		Wohnprojekt Elf Freunde, Berlin
2014	7	Kaiserliches Arbeitshaus, Berlin
2015		Umbau Dresdner Residenzschloss Georgenbau, Dresden
2016		Haus Lindetal, Mecklenburg-Vorpommern
	8	Wettbewerb Alte Akademie, München
		Wettbewerb Viking Age Museum, Oslo (Anerkennung)
2017		Erweiterung Arndt-Gymnasium, Berlin
2018		Programmwettbewerb zur Neuen Bauakademie, Berlin (zusammen mit Ulrich Müller; Preisträger)
	9	*Ambiguous Form Finder*, House of Art, České Budějovice
2019		Haus der Kunst, Gütersloh
		Stadtwerkstatt, Berlin
2020		Wettbewerb Eingang Kyffhäuser Nationaldenkmal (2. Preis)
		Albert-Schweitzer-Schule, Wiesbaden
		Erweiterung Kaiserin-Theophanu-Schule, Köln
		Bürohaus Deutscher Bundestag, Berlin
	10	Wettbewerb Musée Gruérien Bulle, Fribourg (zusammen mit NB.Arch; 3. Preis)
		Sächsische Landesausstellung, Zwickau
		Umbau Hauptgüterbahnhof, Hannover

Bauten in Planung und Ausführung

Spore Initiative, Berlin
Jugendfreizeiteinrichtung Neudecker Weg, Berlin
Haus Gemeinnütziger Journalismus, Berlin
Wohnkomplex Rummelsburger Bucht, Berlin
11 Umbau Kornversuchsspeicher, Berlin
12 Schule Krampnitz, Potsdam
Zentrum für Sprache und Bewegung, Berlin
Lew-Tolstoi-Schule, Berlin

1

2

3

4

5

6

7

8

9

LIST OF WORKS
Selection of buildings, projects and competitions

2000	1	Sequenz, temporary workspace, Weimar
2006	2	Zivcec residential building, Weimar
2008	3	Conversion, Freudenstein Castle, Freiberg
		Terra Mineralia, TU Bergakademie, Freiberg
2010	4	Anna Seghers Interdenominational School, Berlin
		Fichtelberg mountain hut, Tellerhäuser
		Competition, FRG foyer art and exhibition hall, Bonn (1st Prize)
		Competition, rehearsal stage centre, Deutsches Theater, Berlin (2nd Prize)
		Competition, Sprengel Museum extension, Hanover (4th Prize)
2011	5	*In Love, to:*, Deutsches Architektur Zentrum (DAZ), Berlin
	6	Locomotive shed, Wriezener Bahnhof, Berlin
		Competition, Ahlem Memorial, Hanover (2nd Prize)
2012		Ludwig Hoffmann Primary School, Berlin
		St. Petri-Pauli Christening Centre, Lutherstadt Eisleben
		Competition, Archaeological Visitor Centre, Petriplatz, Berlin (2nd Prize)
		Competition, Jewish Museum extension, Frankfurt a.M. (Merit)
2012		*Aviation*, Transport Museum, Dresden
2013		"Elf-Freunde" housing project, Berlin
2014	7	Imperial Workhouse, Berlin
2015		Conversion of the Georgenbau, Royal Palace, Dresden
2016		Lindetal House, Mecklenburg-West Pomerania
	8	Competition, Alte Akademie, Munich
		Competition, Viking Age Museum, Oslo (Merit)
2017		Extension, Arndt grammar school, Berlin
2018		Programme competition, Neue Bauakademie, Berlin (with Ulrich Müller; laureate)
	9	Ambiguous Form Finder, House of Art, České Budějovice
2019		Haus der Kunst, Gütersloh
		Urban workshop, Berlin
2020		Competition, entrance to the Kyffhäuser National Monument (2nd Prize)
		Albert Schweitzer School, Wiesbaden
		Extension, Kaiserin Theophanu School, Cologne
		Office, German Bundestag, Berlin
	10	Competition, Musée Gruérien Bulle, Fribourg (with NB.Arch, 3rd Prize)
		Saxony State Exhibition, Zwickau
		Conversion, Main Freight Station, Hanover

Buildings planned and under construction

Spore Initiative, Berlin
Youth Centre, Neudecker Weg, Berlin
Haus Gemeinnütziger Journalismus, Berlin
Housing complex, Rummelsburger Bucht, Berlin
11 Conversion, Kornversuchsspeicher, Berlin
12 Krampnitz School, Potsdam
Centre for Language and Movement, Berlin
Lew Tolstoi School, Berlin

10

11

12

MARTIN FRÖHLICH

1968	geboren in Magdeburg
1989–1994	Architekturstudium an der Bauhaus-Universität Weimar
Seit 2000	Gründer und Partner von AFF
Seit 2012	Professur an der EPFL Lausanne zusammen mit Anja Fröhlich
	Jurymitglied und Preisrichter bei Wettbewerben und Architekturpreisen

SVEN FRÖHLICH

1974	geboren in Magdeburg
1995–2000	Architektur- und Designstudium an der Bauhaus-Universität Weimar
Seit 2000	Gründer und Partner von AFF
Seit 2018	Mitglied des Gestaltungsbeirats der Stadt Ludwigsburg
	Jurymitglied und Preisrichter bei Wettbewerben und Architekturpreisen
	Vorträge und Gastkritiken an Universitäten und Kulturinstitutionen

ULRIKE DIX

1980	geboren in Chemnitz
1998–2005	Architekturstudium an der Bauhaus-Universität Weimar und UDK Berlin
2006–2010	Mitarbeiterin AFF
2011–2019	Mitarbeiterin und Assozierte bei AFF
Seit 2020	Partnerin bei AFF

MONIC FRAHN

1972	geboren in Weimar
1995–2001	Architekturstudium an der Bauhaus-Universität Weimar
2001–2002	Mitarbeit bei Leonwohlhage, Berlin
2003–2004	Mitarbeit bei Herzog de Meuron, Basel
2005–2019	Mitarbeiterin bei AFF
Seit 2020	Partnerin bei AFF

ASSOZIIERTE   Francesca Boninsegna, Sylvia Brock, Sascha Schulz

TEAM BERLIN   Jonas Aehling, Alexandra Berthold, Katrin Bräutigam, Martin Gille, Marcus Jahnke, Alexa Linde, Agnieszka Malujdy, Andreas Ressel, Sina Riedlinger, Daniela Ruß, Hanno Schröder, Michael Strixner, Julius Titze, Lisa von Wroblewsky

TEAM LAUSANNE   Tiago P. Borges, Anja Fröhlich, Valentino Vitacca

EHEMALIGE   Catherine Arend, Jana Auer, Thomas Barth, Antje Bittorf, Tilman Dorn, Henri Fuchs, Paula Vidal Garcia, Gabriele Gebert, Alexander Georgi, Agnes Hartmann, Kerstin Herget, Stephanie Hirschvogel, Martin Hösl, Nicole Jeltsch, Elena Kasumova, Sebastian Kirsch, Friederike Lange, Mari Proll Lien, Torsten Lockl, Jan Musikowski, Lina Müller, Jasmin Neuhaus, Julia Pachera, Dominique Ramrath, Jutta Roßgotterer, Denise Roth, Michael Schacke, Johannes Schumann, Tilman Siegler, Henriette Spörl, Franziska Sturm, Anastasia Svirski, Wen Wang, Thomas Weisheit, Robert Zeimer

MARTIN FRÖHLICH

1968	Born in Magdeburg
1989–1994	Studied Architecture at the Bauhaus-Universität Weimar
Since 2000	Co-founder and Partner of AFF
Since 2012	Professor at the EPFL Lausanne with Anja Fröhlich
	Jury member and judge for competitions and architectural awards

SVEN FRÖHLICH

1974	Born in Magdeburg
1995–2000	Studied Architecture and Design at the Bauhaus-Universität Weimar
Since 2000	Co-founder and Partner of AFF
Since 2018	Member of the Design Advisory Committee of the City of Ludwigsburg
	Jury member and judge for competitions and architectural awards
	Lectures and guest critiques at universities and cultural institutions

ULRIKE DIX

1980	Born in Chemnitz
1998–2005	Studied Architecture at the Bauhaus-Universität Weimar and the UDK Berlin
2006–2010	Employed at AFF
2011–2019	Employed at and Associated Partner of AFF
Since 2020	Partner of AFF

MONIC FRAHN

1972	Born in Weimar
1995–2001	Studied Architecture at the Bauhaus-Universität Weimar
2001–2002	Employed at Leonwohlhage, Berlin
2003–2004	Employed at Herzog de Meuron, Basel
2005–2019	Employed at AFF
Since 2020	Partner of AFF

ASSOCIATED PARTNERS

Francesca Boninsegna, Sylvia Brock, Sascha Schulz

TEAM BERLIN Jonas Aehling, Alexandra Berthold, Katrin Bräutigam, Martin Gille, Marcus Jahnke, Alexa Linde, Agnieszka Malujdy, Andreas Ressel, Sina Riedlinger, Daniela Ruß, Hanno Schröder, Michael Strixner, Julius Titze, Lisa von Wroblewsky

TEAM LAUSANNE Tiago P. Borges, Anja Fröhlich, Valentino Vitacca

FORMER EMPLOYEES

Catherine Arend, Jana Auer, Thomas Barth, Antje Bittorf, Tilman Dorn, Henri Fuchs, Paula Vidal Garcia, Gabriele Gebert, Alexander Georgi, Agnes Hartmann, Kerstin Herget, Stephanie Hirschvogel, Martin Hösl, Nicole Jeltsch, Elena Kasumova, Sebastian Kirsch, Friederike Lange, Mari Proll Lien, Torsten Lockl, Jan Musikowski, Lina Müller, Jasmin Neuhaus, Julia Pachera, Dominique Ramrath, Jutta Roßgotterer, Denise Roth, Michael Schacke, Johannes Schumann, Tilman Siegler, Henriette Spörl, Franziska Sturm, Anastasia Svirski, Wen Wang, Thomas Weisheit, Robert Zeimer

BIBLIOGRAFIE (Auswahl seit 2010)

2010
«Cabana encofrada» [Schutzhütte]. In: Arquitectura Viva, Nr. 139, S. 62–65
Florian Heilmeyer: «AFF preserves its childhood memories in concrete» [Schutzhütte]. In: MARK, Nr. 26, S. 62–63
Jan Esche: «Architektur als Trumpf» [Schloss Freudenstein]. In: HotelMOSAIK, Sommerausgabe, S. 20–22
«Hütte im Erzgebirge». In: Detail, Nr. 7/8, S. 718–721
Kaye Geipel: «Lust an der Schwere» [Schutzhütte]. In: Bauwelt, Nr. 11, S. 24–31
Douglas Murphy: «This mountain hut hides a ghostly secret». In: icon, Nr. 9, S. 48–52
«Fichtelberg Mountain hut». In: Architecture today, Nr. 5, S. 21
Alexander Hosch: «Renaissance im Erzgebirge». In: AD, Nr. 10, S. 60–65
«Hüttenzauber». In: AIT, Nr. 4, S. 18
Ioana Păunescu: «Schloss Freudenstein». In: Igloo, Nr. 103/104, S. 110–115
«Freudenstein castle». In: MONITOR, Nr. 60, S. 98–103
«Out of the woods» [Schutzhütte]. In: Wallpaper, Nr. 11, S. 94–95
«Rough but ready» [Schutzhütte]. In: A10, Nr. 33, S. 6
Frank Peter Jäger: «Renaissance der Wunderkammer» [Schloss Freudenstein]. In: Ders. (Hrsg.): Alt & Neu – Entwurfshandbuch Bauen im Bestand. Basel, S. 178–181

2011
Martin Fröhlich: «Hutznhaisl» [Schutzhütte]. In: ABITARE, Nr. 6, S. 80–87
«Anna Seghers School». In: The architectural rewiew, Nr. 3, S. 56–61
«Ein Platz an der Sonne» [Gemeinschaftsschule Anna Seghers]. In: ELLE Decoration, Nr. 3, S. 26
Florian Heilmeyer: «Der Zauber der Dinge» [diverse Projekte]. In: werk, bauen+wohnen, Nr. 6, S. 14–21
Mathias Remmele: «Fassadenrecycling» [Schutzhütte]. In: Archithese, Nr. 2, S. 62–65
«Objekthaftigkeit und Materialechtheit» [Interview mit AFF]. In: Colore, Nr. 4, S. 4–11
«Mit dem Körper denken» [zur Ausstellung im DAZ Berlin]. In: trans, 19. September, S. 92–95
«In Love, to:» [zur Ausstellung im DAZ Berlin]. In: Bauwelt, Nr. 10, S. 4
«Maxime des Elementaren» [Interview zur Schutzhütte am Fichtelberg]. In: Betonprisma, Nr. 92, S. 19
«Mit dem Körper denken» [zur Ausstellung im DAZ Berlin]. In: Bauwelt, Nr. 14, S. 26–31
«Schule in Berlin» [Gemeinschaftsschule Anna Seghers]. In: Detail, Nr. 7/8, S. 875–879
«Kosmos – Erster Schnee» [Schutzhütte]. In: Süddeutsche Zeitung Magazin, Nr. 45, S. 11
Sebastian Redecke: «Netzmuster als Hülle» [Gemeinschaftsschule Anna Seghers]. In: Bauwelt, Nr. 3, S. 12–19
«Gemeinschaftsschule Anna Seghers» und «Schloss Freudenstein». In: Ecola 2011. Leinfelden-Echterdingen, S. 98–99, 174–175
«Umbau und Erweiterung Schloss Freudenstein» und «Schützhütte am Fichtelberg». In: BDA (Hrsg.): Architektur in Sachsen – Zeitgenössisches Bauen seit 1991. Leipzig, S. 14–15, S. 22–23

2012
Oliver Elser: «AFF Architekten – Schutzhütte». In: Peter Cachola Schmal (Hrsg.): Deutsches Architektur Jahrbuch 2011/12. München, S. 34–45
«AFF ‹Hutznhaisl›» [Schutzhütte]. In: Architecture Now, Nr. 8, S. 70–75
«Schule in Berlin» [Gemeinschaftsschule Anna Seghers]. In: Christian Schittich (Hrsg.): Einfach Bauen. Zwei. München, S. 150–153
«Schutzhütte am Fichtelberg». In: Muck Petzet / Florian Heilmeyer (Hrsg.): Reduce Reuse Recycle. Berlin, S. 186–189
«AFF Architekten». In: Salvatore Spataro (Hrsg.): what's up? – 15 Young European Architects. Siracusa, S. 14–25
«Fichtelberg Mountain Hut». In: Virginia McLeod: Detail in Contemporary Concrete Architecture. London, S. 76–79
«Ludwig-Hoffmann-Grundschule». In: Architektenkammer Berlin (Hrsg.): Architektur Berlin – Baukultur in und aus der Hauptstadt (Band 2). Salenstein, S. 110–111
«AFF architekten». In: A+U, Nr. 508, S. 104–107
«Hut on Fichtelberg mountain». In: A+U, Nr. 499, S. 16–25
Kirsten Klingbeil: «Übergießen, Ein- oder Untertauchen» [Taufzentrum St. Petri-Pauli]. In: Bauwelt, Nr. 26, S. 18–19

2013
«Teilumbau der Freiligrath-Schule zur Ganztagsschule». In: Bauwelt, Nr. 27/28, S. 26–27
«ELFFREUNDE». In: Kristien Ring et al. (Hrsg.): Selfmade City. Berlin, S. 172–173
Christoph Tempel: «Lokschuppen Wriezener Bahnhof». In: Bauwelt Nr. 47, S. 26–29

2014
Christian Tröster: «Viel aus Wenig» [AFF]. In: Architektur & Wohnen, Nr. 1, S. 112–115
«Hut in Fichtelberg – AFF architekten». In: C3, Nr. 353, S. 24–35
Christina Gräwe: «Ohne Reibung keine Wärme – Die AFF-Familie». In: KAP, Nr. 8, S. 47–53

2015
«AFF ‹Hutzenhaisl›». In: Philipp Jodidio: 100 Contemporary Green Buildings. Köln, S. 32–37
«Wohnprojekt in Berlin» [Elf Freunde]. In: ECOLA 2015. Leinfelden-Echterdingen, S. 150–151
«Stadthäuser Baugruppe Elf Freunde, Berlin». In: Peter Cachola Schmal (Hrsg.): Deutsches Architektur Jahrbuch 2015/16. München, S. 34–39
«Schule in Berlin» [Gemeinschaftsschule Anna Seghers]. In: Best of DETAIL – Fassaden. München, S. 123–125
«AFF». In: Arkitektur, Nr. 3, S. 82–89
«El Pasado presente» [Schutzhütte]. In: summa +, Nr. 142, S. 58–61
«Schutzhütte am Fichtelberg». In: Marion von der Heyde: Gestalten mit Beton. Köln, S. 78

2016
«Kaiserliches Arbeitshaus Rummelsburg». In: Architektenkammer Berlin (Hrsg.): Architektur Berlin – Baukultur in und aus der Hauptstadt (Band 5). Salenstein, S. 28–29
«Anna-Seghers-Schule». In: Best of DETAIL – Bauen für Kinder. München, S. 119–121
«Sankt Petri-Pauli Church». In: Mark Magazine, Nr. 59, S. 80–81
Martin Fröhlich: «Von Hofgeschichte und Stadttexturen» [Ludwig-Hoffmann-Grundschule]. In: Schulbau – Bauen für die Bildung, Nr. 1, S. 26–27
«Zukunft im Rückspiegel» [Haus Zivec]. In: 100 Deutsche Häuser, Nr. 16, S. 84

2017
Michael Kasiske: «Voll Holz» [Haus Lindetal]. In: Bauwelt, Nr. 8, S. 31
«Kunst Werk» [Haus Lindetal]. In: 100 Ferienhäuser, S. 16
«Sprengelmuseum», «Grimmwelt» und «Bauhausarchiv». In: Grundrissfibel Museumsbauten. Zürich, S. 224–225, S. 386–387, S. 488–489
«Ornament und Konstruktion. Architektur und Handwerk. Tradition und Zukunft» [Haus Lindetal]. In: Häuser des Jahres 2017. München, S. 224–229

BIBLIOGRAPHY (selection since 2010)

2010
"Cabana encofrada" [Mountain hut, Fichtelberg]. In: *Arquitectura Viva*, No. 139, p. 62–65
Florian Heilmeyer: "AFF preserves its childhood memories in concrete" [Mountain hut, Fichtelberg]. In: *MARK*, No. 26, p. 62–63
Jan Esche: "Architektur als Trumpf" [Schloss Freudenstein]. In: *HotelMOSAIK*, Summer Issue, p. 20–22
"Hütte im Erzgebirge". In: *Detail*, No. 7/8, p. 718–721
Kaye Geipel: "Lust an der Schwere" [Mountain hut, Fichtelberg]. In: *Bauwelt*, No. 11, p. 24–31
Douglas Murphy: "This mountain hut hides a ghostly secret". In: *icon*, No. 9, p. 48–52
"Fichtelberg Mountain hut". In: *Architecture today*, No. 5, p. 21
Alexander Hosch: "Renaissance im Erzgebirge". In: *AD*, No. 10, p. 60–65
"Hüttenzauber". In: *AIT*, No. 4, p. 18
Ioana Păunescu: "Schloss Freudenstein". In: *Igloo*, No. 103/104, p. 110–115
"Freudenstein castle". In: *MONITOR*, No. 60, p. 98–103
"Out of the woods" [Mountain hut, Fichtelberg]. In: *Wallpaper*, No. 11, p. 94–95
"Rough but ready" [Mountain hut, Fichtelberg]. In: *A10*, No. 33, p. 6
Frank Peter Jäger: "Renaissance der Wunderkammer" [Schloss Freudenstein]. In: id. (Ed.): *Alt & Neu – Entwurfshandbuch Bauen im Bestand*. Basel, p. 178–181

2011
Martin Fröhlich: "Hutznhaisl" [Mountain hut, Fichtelberg]. In: *ABITARE*, No. 6, p. 80–87
"Anna Seghers School". In: *The architectural review*, No. 3, p. 56–61
"Ein Platz an der Sonne" [Anna Seghers School]. In: *ELLE Decoration*, No. 3, p. 26
Florian Heilmeyer: "Der Zauber der Dinge" [various projects]. In: *werk, bauen+wohnen*, No. 6, p. 14–21
Mathias Remmele: "Fassadenrecycling" [Mountain hut, Fichtelberg]. In: *Archithese*, No. 2, p. 62–65
"Objekthaftigkeit und Materialechtheit" [Interview with AFF]. In: *Colore*, No. 4, p. 4–11
"Mit dem Körper denken" [Exhibition at the DAZ Berlin]. In: *trans*, September 19, p. 92–95
"In Love, to:" [Exhibition at the DAZ Berlin]. In: *Bauwelt*, No. 10, p. 4
"Maxime des Elementaren" [Interview on the mountain hut, Fichtelberg]. In: *Betonprisma*, No. 92, p. 19
"Mit dem Körper denken" [Exhibition at the DAZ Berlin]. In: *Bauwelt*, No. 14, p. 26–31
"Schule in Berlin" [Anna Seghers School]. In: *Detail*, No. 7/8, p. 875–879
"Kosmos – Erster Schnee" [Mountain hut, Fichtelberg]. In: *Süddeutsche Zeitung Magazin*, No. 45, p. 11
Sebastian Redecke: "Netzmuster als Hülle" [Anna Seghers School]. In: *Bauwelt*, No. 3, p. 12–19
"Gemeinschaftsschule Anna Seghers" and "Schloss Freudenstein". In: *Ecola* 2011. Leinfelden-Echterdingen, p. 98–99, 174–175
"Umbau und Erweiterung Schloss Freudenstein" and "Schützhütte am Fichtelberg". In: BDA (Ed.): *Architektur in Sachsen – Zeitgenössisches Bauen seit 1991*. Leipzig, p. 14–15, p. 22–23

2012
Oliver Elser: "AFF Architekten – Schutzhütte". In: Peter Cachola Schmal (Ed.): *Deutsches Architektur Jahrbuch 2011/12*. Munich, p. 34–45
"AFF 'Hutznhaisl'". In: *Architecture Now*, No. 8, p. 70–75
"Schule in Berlin" [Gemeinschaftsschule Anna Seghers]. In: Christian Schittich (Ed.): *Einfach Bauen. Zwei*. Munich, p. 150–153
"Schutzhütte am Fichtelberg". In: Muck Petzet / Florian Heilmeyer (Eds.): *Reduce Reuse Recycle*. Berlin, p. 186–189
"AFF Architekten". In: Salvatore Spataro (Ed.): *what's up – 15 Young European Architects*. Siracusa, p. 14–25
"Fichtelberg Mountain Hut". In: Virginia McLeod: *Detail in Contemporary Concrete Architecture*. London, p. 76–79
"Ludwig-Hoffmann-Grundschule". In: Architektenkammer Berlin (Ed.): *Architektur Berlin – Baukultur in und aus der Hauptstadt* (Vol. 2). Salenstein, p. 110–111
"AFF architekten". In: *A+U*, No. 508, p. 104–107
"Hut on Fichtelberg mountain". In: *A+U*, No. 499, p. 16–25
Kirsten Klingbeil: "Übergießen, Ein- oder Untertauchen" [St. Petri-Pauli christening centre]. In: *Bauwelt*, No. 26, p. 18–19

2013
"Teilumbau der Freiligrath-Schule zur Ganztagsschule". In: *Bauwelt*, No. 27/28, p. 26–27
"ELFFREUNDE". In: Kristien Ring et al. (Eds.): *Selfmade City*. Berlin, p. 172–173
Christoph Tempel: "Lokschuppen Wriezener Bahnhof". In: *Bauwelt* No. 47, p. 26–29

2014
Christian Tröster: "Viel aus Wenig" [AFF]. In: *Architektur & Wohnen*, No. 1, p. 112–115
"Hut in Fichtelberg – AFF architekten". In: *C3*, No. 353, p. 24–35
Christina Gräwe: "Ohne Reibung keine Wärme – Die AFF-Familie". In: *KAP*, No. 8, p. 47–53

2015
"AFF 'Hutzenhaisl'". In: Philipp Jodidio: *100 Contemporary Green Buildings*. Cologne, p. 32–37
"Wohnprojekt in Berlin" [Elf Freunde]. In: *ECOLA 2015*. Leinfelden-Echterdingen, p. 150–151
"Stadthäuser Baugruppe Elf Freunde, Berlin". In: Peter Cachola Schmal (Ed.): *Deutsches Architektur Jahrbuch 2015/16*. Munich, p. 34–39
"Schule in Berlin" [Anna Seghers School]. In: *Best of DETAIL – Fassaden*. Munich, p. 123–125
"AFF". In: *Arkitektur*, No. 3, p. 82–89
"El Pasado presente" [mountain hut, Fichtelberg]. In: *summa +*, No. 142, p. 58–61
"Schutzhütte am Fichtelberg". In: Marion von der Heyde: *Gestalten mit Beton*. Cologne, p. 78

2016
"Kaiserliches Arbeitshaus Rummelsburg". In: Architektenkammer Berlin (Ed.): *Architektur Berlin – Baukultur in und aus der Hauptstadt* (Band 5). Salenstein, p. 28–29
"Anna-Seghers-Schule". In: *Best of DETAIL – Bauen für Kinder*. Munich, p. 119–121
"Sankt Petri-Pauli Church". In: *Mark Magazine*, No. 59, p. 80–81
Martin Fröhlich: "Von Hofgeschichte und Stadttexturen" [Ludwig Hoffmann Primary School]. In: *Schulbau – Bauen für die Bildung*, No. 1, p. 26–27
"Zukunft im Rückspiegel" [Zivcec House]. In: *100 Deutsche Häuser*, No. 16, p. 84

2017
Michael Kasiske: "Voll Holz" [Lindetal House]. In: *Bauwelt*, No. 8, p. 31
"Kunst Werk" [Lindetal House]. In: *100 Ferienhäuser*, p. 16
"Sprengelmuseum", "Grimmwelt" and "Bauhausarchiv". In: *Grundrissfibel Museumsbauten*. Zurich, p. 224–225, p. 386–387, p. 488–489

2018	«Erweiterungsbau Arndt-Gymnasium». In: Bauwelt, Nr. 2, S. 32–35 Kirsten Klingbeil: «Nach Maß und in Serie. Schulen von AFF Architekten […]». In: Bauwelt, Nr. 18, S. 22–29 «Lokschuppen Wriezener Bahnhof». In: A+U 551, S. 184 «Haus Lindetal». In: Architektenkammer Berlin (Hrsg.): Architektur Berlin – Baukultur in und aus der Hauptstadt (Band 7). Salenstein, S. 50–51
2019	«Harbour, Playground, Zoo. The School as City Space». In: Francesca Ferguson / Make_Shift (Hrsg.): Make City. A Compendium of Urban Alternatives. Berlin, S. 176–181 «Erweiterung Arndt-Gymnasium». In: Yorck Förster et al. (Hrsg.): Architekturführer Deutschland 2019. Berlin, S. 74–75 «Ludwig-Hoffmann-Grundschule» und «Gemeinschaftsschule Anna Seghers». In: Sibylle Kramer: Building to educate. Salenstein, S. 20–23 und S. 174–175 «Haus Lindetal». In: Hartwig Schneider / Uwe Schröder (Hrsg.): Identität der Architektur. 2: Material. Köln, S. 30–33 «Erweiterung Arndt-Gymnasium». In: Architektenkammer Berlin (Hrsg.): Architektur Berlin – Baukultur in und aus der Hauptstadt (Band 8). Salenstein, S. 124–125 Gisela Gary: «Raffiniert weitergebaut. Arndt-Gymnasium Berlin». In: Beton Zement, Nr. 4, S. 40–41 Hartmut Möller: «Vom Abstellgleis geholt. Ehemaliger Hauptgüterbahnhof Hannover». In: DB, Nr. 12, S. 115 Juliane von Hagen: «Back on Track» [Hauptgüterbahnhof]. In: Garten und Landschaft, Nr. 11, S. 42–47 Benedikt Crone: «Durchgezogen» [Hauptgüterbahnhof]. In: Bauwelt, Nr. 24, S. 38–45 «AFFs sentimentale Objekte». In: Eva Maria Froschauer: Entwurfsdinge – Vom Sammeln als Werkzeug moderner Architektur. Basel, S. 342–371 «In Love, to: Geliebte, gesammelte Dinge in der architektonischen Praxis». In: Eva Maria Froschauer: Entwurfsdinge – Vom Sammeln als Werkzeug moderner Architektur. Basel, S. 245–261
2020	«Stadtwerkstatt». In: Architektenkammer Berlin (Hrsg.): Architektur Berlin – Building Berlin (Band 9). Salenstein, S. 120–121

AUSSTELLUNGEN

2018	*Ambiguous Form Finder*, House of Art, České Budějovice
2017	*Steal Schinkel*, Satellit – Architektur Galerie Berlin *This is!*, AFF-Atelier, Berlin
2016	*Affairs*, Galerie Domino, Straßburg
2012	*Reduce/Reuse/Recycle – Architecture as Resource*, Architekturbiennale Venedig
2011	*In Love, to:*, Deutsches Architektur Zentrum, Berlin
2009	*Teile zum Ganzen – An Aggregate Body*, Architektur Galerie Werkraum, Berlin

PREISE

2018	BDA Preis Berlin: Elf Freunde, Berlin Heinze ArchitektenAWARD: Haus Lindetal, Mecklenburg-Vorpommern
2017	Sächsischer Staatspreis für Baukultur (Anerkennung): Umbau Schloss Freudenstein
2016	Deutscher Bauherrenpreis: Elf Freunde, Berlin Heinze ArchitektenAWARD: Kaiserliches Arbeitshaus, Berlin Deutscher Holzbaupreis: Haus Lindetal, Mecklenburg-Vorpommern
2014	«Respekt und Perspektive» – Bauen im Bestand Preis: Kaiserliches Arbeitshaus, Berlin
2013	Architekturpreis Sachsen-Anhalt: Taufzentrum, Lutherstadt Eisleben BDA-Preis Sachsen, Schutzhütte, Tellerhäuser
2012	Schelling Architekturpreis (Nominierung)
2010	BDA Preis Sachsen: Umbau Schloss Freudenstein
2008	Architekturpreis Beton: Umbau Schloss Freudenstein
2006	Weissenhof Architekturförderpreis: Neues Bauen am Horn, Weimar Deutscher Bauherrenpreis: 4 Gleiche – Neues Bauen am Horn, Weimar
2005	Europäischer Kalksandsteinpreis: 4 Gleiche – Neues Bauen am Horn, Weimar
2001	Thüringer Wohnungsbaupreis (Anerkennung): Haus Ihlenfeldt, Weimar Architekturpreis Sachsen-Anhalt (Anerkennung): Altenpflegeheim, Schwanebeck

HANS-CHRISTIAN SCHINK (FOTOS)

*1961 in Erfurt, lebt in Mecklenburg. 1986–1991 Studium der Fotografie und 1993 Meisterschülerabschluss an der HGB Leipzig. Er erhielt mehrere Stipendien und Preise, u.a. Stipendium der Villa Massimo, Deutsche Akademie Rom (2014); Villa Kamogawa, Goethe Institut Kyoto (2012). Publikation diverser Monografien, u.a.: *Hinterland* (2020), *Burma* (2018), *Kochi Nights* (2018), *Fotografien aus Rom* (2015), *Tōhoku* (2013), *Fläming* (2012), *Hans-Christian Schink* (2011).

HARTMUT FRANK (TEXTBEITRAG)

*1942, lebt in Hamburg. Architekt, Dipl.-Ing. (TU Berlin), Professor emeritus der HafenCity Universität Hamburg. Er unterrichtete Geschichte und Theorie der Architektur an diversen Universitäten in Europa und Amerika, zuletzt am Politecnico di Milano. Er forschte und publizierte zu Fragen der Architektur und des Städtebaus in der europäischen Baukultur, insbesondere zum Verhältnis von Architektur und Politik. Hierzu betreute er eine Reihe von thematischen Ausstellungen, die zum Teil weltweit präsentiert wurden.

2017	"Ornament und Konstruktion. Architektur und Handwerk. Tradition und Zukunft" [Lindetal House]. In: *Häuser des Jahres 2017*. Munich, p. 224–229
2018	"Erweiterungsbau Arndt-Gymnasium". In: *Bauwelt*, No. 2, p. 32–35 Kirsten Klingbeil: "Nach Maß und in Serie. Schulen von AFF Architekten [...]". In: *Bauwelt*, No. 18, p. 22–29 "Lokschuppen Wriezener Bahnhof". In: *A+U* 551, p. 184 "Haus Lindetal". In: Architektenkammer Berlin (Ed.): *Architektur Berlin – Baukultur in und aus der Hauptstadt* (Band 7). Salenstein, p. 50–51
2019	Anja Fröhlich: "Harbour, Playground, Zoo. The School as City Space". In: Francesca Ferguson / Make_Shift (Eds.): *Make City. A Compendium of Urban Alternatives*. Berlin, p. 176–181 "Erweiterung Arndt-Gymnasium". In: Yorck Förster et al. (Eds.): *Architekturführer Deutschland 2019*. Berlin, p. 74–75 "Ludwig-Hoffmann-Grundschule" and "Gemeinschaftsschule Anna Seghers". In: Sibylle Kramer: *Building to educate*. Salenstein, p. 20–23 and p. 174–175 "Haus Lindetal". In: Hartwig Schneider / Uwe Schröder (Eds.): *Identität der Architektur. 2: Material*. Cologne, p. 30–33 "Erweiterung Arndt-Gymnasium". In: Architektenkammer Berlin (Ed.): *Architektur Berlin – Baukultur in und aus der Hauptstadt* (Band 8). Salenstein, p. 124–125 Gisela Gary: "Raffiniert weitergebaut. Arndt-Gymnasium Berlin". In: *Beton Zement*, No. 4, p. 40–41 Hartmut Möller: "Vom Abstellgleis geholt. Ehemaliger Hauptgüterbahnhof Hannover". In: *DB*, No. 12, p. 115 Juliane von Hagen: "Back on Track" [Hanover Main Freight Railway Station]. In: *Garten und Landschaft*, No. 11, p. 42–47 Benedikt Crone: "Durchgezogen" [Hanover Main Freight Railway Station]. In: *Bauwelt*, No. 24, p. 38–45 "AFFs sentimentale Objekte". In: Eva Maria Froschauer: *Entwurfsdinge – Vom Sammeln als Werkzeug moderner Architektur*. Basel, p. 342–371 "In Love, to: Geliebte, gesammelte Dinge in der architektonischen Praxis". In: Eva Maria Froschauer: *Entwurfsdinge – Vom Sammeln als Werkzeug moderner Architektur*. Basel, p. 245–261
2020	"Stadtwerkstatt". In: Architektenkammer Berlin (Ed.): *Architektur Berlin – Building Berlin* (Band 9). Salenstein, p. 120–121

EXHIBITIONS

2018	*Ambiguous Form Finder*, House of Art, České Budějovice
2017	*Steal Schinkel, Satellit* – Architektur Galerie Berlin *This is!*, AFF-Atelier, Berlin
2016	*Affairs*, Galerie Domino, Strasbourg
2012	*Reduce/Reuse/Recycle – Architecture as Resource*, Venice Biennale of Architecture
2011	*In Love, to:* – Deutsches Architektur Zentrum, Berlin
2009	*Teile zum Ganzen – An Aggregate Body*, Architektur Galerie Werkraum, Berlin

AWARDS

2018	BDA Preis Berlin: Elf Freunde, Berlin Heinze ArchitektenAWARD: Haus Lindetal, Mecklenburg-Vorpommern
2017	Sächsischer Staatspreis für Baukultur (Commendation): Conversion, Schloss Freudenstein
2016	Deutscher Bauherrenpreis: Elf Freunde, Berlin Heinze ArchitektenAWARD: Kaiserliches Arbeitshaus, Berlin Deutscher Holzbaupreis: Haus Lindetal, Mecklenburg-Vorpommern
2014	"Respekt und Perspektive" – Bauen im Bestand Preis: Kaiserliches Arbeitshaus, Berlin
2013	Architekturpreis Sachsen-Anhalt: Christening centre, Eisleben BDA-Preis Sachsen, mountain hut, Tellerhäuser
2012	Nomination, Schelling Architekturpreis
2010	BDA Preis Sachsen: Conversion, Schloss Freudenstein
2008	Architekturpreis Beton: Conversion, Schloss Freudenstein
2006	Weissenhof Architekturförderpreis: Neues Bauen am Horn, Weimar Deutscher Bauherrenpreis: 4 equal prizes – Neues Bauen am Horn, Weimar
2005	Europäischer Kalksandsteinpreis: 4 equal prizes – Neues Bauen am Horn, Weimar
2001	Thüringer Wohnungsbaupreis (Commendation): Haus Ihlenfeldt, Weimar Architekturpreis Sachsen-Anhalt (Commendation): Nursing home for the elderly, Schwanebeck

HANS-CHRISTIAN SCHINK (PHOTOGRAPHY)

Born in Erfurt in 1961, lives in Mecklenburg. 1986–1991 studied Photography, 1993 Master-Student graduation at the HGB Leipzig. Several scholarships and prizes, including Villa Massimo, Deutsche Akademie Rom (2014); Villa Kamogawa, Goethe Institut Kyoto (2012). Published various monographs, including: *Hinterland* (2020), *Burma* (2018), *Kochi Nights* (2018), *Fotografien aus Rom* (2015), *Tōhoku* (2013), *Fläming* (2012), *Hans-Christian Schink* (2011).

HARTMUT FRANK (ARTICLE)

Born in 1942, lives in Hamburg. Architect, Dipl.-Ing. (TU Berlin), Professor emeritus, HafenCity Universität Hamburg. Taught History and Theory of Architecture at various universities in Europe and America, most recently at the Politecnico di Milano. Research and publications on aspects of architecture and urban planning in European building culture, especially on the relationship between architecture and politics. In this context, he supervised a series of thematic exhibitions, including presentations around the world.

FINANZIELLE UND IDEELLE UNTERSTÜTZUNG

Ein besonderer Dank gilt den Institutionen und Sponsorfirmen, deren finanzielle Unterstützungen wesentlich zum Entstehen dieser Buchreihe beitragen. Ihr kulturelles Engagement ermöglicht ein fruchtbares und freundschaftliches Zusammenwirken von Baukultur und Bauwirtschaft.

FINANCIAL AND CONCEPTUAL SUPPORT

Special thanks to our sponsors and institutions whose financial support has helped us so much with the production of this series of books. Their cultural commitment is a valuable contribution to fruitful and cordial collaboration between the culture and economics of architecture.

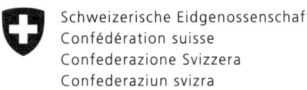

Schweizerische Eidgenossenschaft   Eidgenössisches Departement des Innern EDI
Confédération suisse   Département fédéral de l'intérieur DFI
Confederazione Svizzera   Dipartimento federale dell'interno DFI
Confederaziun svizra   Departament federal da l'intern DFI
                                    Bundesamt für Kultur BAK
                                    Office fédéral de la culture OFC
                                    Ufficio federale della cultura UFC
                                    Uffizi federal da cultura UFC

SCHNETZER PUSKAS
INGENIEURE

Schöpflin Stiftung

AFF – Berlin/Lausanne
21. Band der Reihe De aedibus international
Herausgeber: Heinz Wirz, Luzern
Konzept: Heinz Wirz; AFF, Berlin/Lausanne
Projektleitung: Quart Verlag, Linus Wirz
Textbeitrag: Hartmut Frank, Hamburg
Objekttexte: AFF, Anja Fröhlich
Textlektorat Deutsch: Miriam Seifert-Waibel, Hamburg
Übersetzung Deutsch–Englisch: Benjamin Liebelt, Berlin
Fotos: Hans-Christian Schink, Berlin; ausser:
Frank-Heinrich Müller, Leipzig S. 35
Redesign: BKVK, Basel – Beat Keusch, Angelina Köpplin-Stützle
Grafische Umsetzung: Quart Verlag; Caroline Reichardt, Berlin
Lithos: Printeria, Luzern
Druck: Printer Trento S.R.L., Trient

© Copyright 2020
Quart Verlag Luzern, Heinz Wirz
Alle Rechte vorbehalten
ISBN 978-3-03761-241-5

AFF – Berlin/Lausanne
Volume 21 of the series De aedibus international
Edited by: Heinz Wirz, Lucerne
Concept: Heinz Wirz; AFF, Berlin/Lausanne
Project management: Quart Verlag, Linus Wirz
Article by: Hartmut Frank, Hamburg
Project descriptions: AFF, Anja Fröhlich
German text editing: Miriam Seifert-Waibel, Hamburg
English translation: Benjamin Liebelt, Berlin
Photos: Hans-Christian Schink, Berlin; except:
Frank-Heinrich Müller, Leipzig p. 35
Redesign: BKVK, Basel – Beat Keusch,
Angelina Köpplin-Stützle
Graphical layout: Quart Verlag; Caroline Reichardt, Berlin
Lithos: Printeria, Lucerne
Printing: Printer Trento S.R.L., Trento

© Copyright 2020
Quart Verlag Luzern, Heinz Wirz
All rights reserved
ISBN 978-3-03761-241-5

Quart Verlag GmbH
Denkmalstrasse 2, CH-6006 Luzern
books@quart.ch, www.quart.ch

De aedibus international
Zeitgenössische Architekten und ihre Bauten

De aedibus international
Contemporary architects and their buildings

21	AFF – Berlin/Lausanne (de/en)	11	Uwe Schröder – Bonn (de/en)
20	Onsitestudio – Mailand/Milan (de/en)	10	Stephen Taylor Architects – London (de/en)
19	a2o architecten – Brüssel/Hasselt (de/en)	9	Titus Bernhard Architekten – Augsburg (de/en)
18	Schulz und Schulz – Leipzig (de/en)	8	Dietrich|Untertrifaller – Bregenz (de/en)
17	bernardo bader architekten – Bregenz (de/en)	7	Geurst & Schulze Architecten – Den Haag (de/en)
16	Schenker Salvi Weber – Wien (de/en)	6	Wingender Hovenier Architecten – Amsterdam (de/en)
15	Henley Halebrown – London (de/en)	5	Tony Fretton Architects – London (de/en)
14	Walter Angonese – Kaltern/Caldaro (de/en)	4	Jonathan Woolf Architects – London (de/en)
13	architecten de vylder vinck taillieu – Gent (de/en)	3	Hufnagel Pütz Rafaelian – Berlin (de/en)
12	De Smet Vermeulen architecten – Gent (de/en; nl/fr)	2	Hild und K – München (de/en)
		1	Stanton Williams – London (de/en)

books@quart.ch, www.quart.ch